LADIES

Better

Understanding

God

Book One

Lady BUGS... The Journey Begins

DENELL DENNIS

Cover art and design by Amy Allison.
Custom Lady BUG artwork by Beverly Richey.

IISBN-13: 978-0-89098-425-3
ISBN-10: 0-89098-425-5

In Memory of...
The First Lady BUG, Carrie Elliott

In the fall of 2003, Carrie Elliott and a group of ladies from her church in Montgomery, Alabama planned a ladies retreat. Carrie came up with a "Lady BUG" theme, an acronym for Ladies Better Understanding God. Months later my brother's wife, Carol, who had attended the retreat, gave me the idea. My heart is sad that Carrie died before I ever had a chance to meet her. Fortunately, through a series of events only God could have orchestrated, I have had the honor of meeting Carrie's dear friend, Sherry. These words were written by Sherry in memory of her precious sister in Christ.

Each of us has her own garden: a ladies group at church, a neighborhood Bible study; or a group of friends. Wherever your garden grows, there are special Lady BUGs tending to every need. God placed them there to help you better understand Him. Not long ago, I found myself asking, "Why was my dear friend and mentor, the first Lady BUG, plucked from my garden?"

I am blessed to have known Carrie Elliott, who created the original Lady BUG idea. I met Carrie the first night I attended our new church in the Ladies Bible Class on Wednesday night in 1996. It only took a few words from this Lady BUG Sister to make me feel right at home. After class, I thanked her for the lesson in which she used a pink rose from her garden as an illustration. With a smile that could warm a winter's day she placed the pink rose in my hand. Her words were kind and filled with love. I told her it was my birthday and she hugged me. That was the beginning of a friendship that grew to sisterhood. I would find myself in the years to come under her Lady BUG wing even when I didn't realize she was there to guide me.

Carrie was a writer only published through her poems. She always wanted to write a book that would help her sisters better understand God as she had come to know Him. However, God had another plan. Carrie battled with cancer and was taken home to be with the Lord. It was only after her body was defeated by cancer that I began to understand God plucking my first Lady BUG Sister from my garden. I know there are many reasons God must have had to bring Carrie home so early in life. I discovered my reason in Auburn, Alabama in February of 2006 at our ladies retreat when I walked into the room set up for our guest speaker. Ladybugs danced across each table and all around the room. There were ladybugs everywhere! That night I was blessed to meet Denell Dennis, the second Lady BUG planned for my garden. I felt Carrie's spirit that night still mentoring me from heaven. Many tears watered the garden that evening when two new Lady Bug Sisters came together.

This Bible Study "Ladies Better Understanding God" is like bread sent from heaven. Come see for yourself how God still moves in His garden today!

Sherry DeBray
Author/Speaker/Lady Bug Sister

Table of Contents

My Purpose for Ladies Better Understanding God

Dear Lady BUG Sister,
Welcome to the garden! My emotions run the gamut as I invite you on this journey with me. In book one of this series, *Lady BUGs...The Journey Begins,* we will seek to better understand God by learning life lessons from "Trail Blazers" in the Word who have gone on before us! Some of these Trail Blazers include Moses, Mary (the Original Lady BUG), David, Mary Magdalene and others. I am borrowing my purpose for this Bible Study from Paul's wonderful letter to the Colossians. Paul's compassion for the believers in Colosse and Laodicea touches me deeply. Read Colossians 2:2-3 in the NIV Bible.

My purpose is that YOU may:

Be encouraged in heart.
Be united in love.
Have the full riches of complete understanding.
Know the mystery of God, namely Christ!
Find the treasures of wisdom and knowledge hidden in Christ.

Sometimes - let's face it – we need some encouragement! Lean in so you can hear me whisper in your ear. This Bible Study is all about ENCOURAGEMENT FOR YOUR HEART! If you're holding this book and reading these words, please know that I have been praying for YOU! It is my sincere prayer that you and I may be "mutually encouraged by each other's faith!" (Romans 1:12) I've also been praying daily that God will give us a spirit of unity as we seek to better understand His will for our lives. We will never completely understand everything there is to know about God. There are more "treasures" to find than we can even fathom! This Bible Study is a journey – a PERSONAL journey – toward better understanding God. Every day we learn a little more than we knew before!

Traveling Tips for Your Journey

Lady BUG Trails

You will notice extra writing space in the margin of every workbook page. These have been placed there for a special reason. Throughout the Bible Study you will find many opportunities to veer off the path we're on and take your own "Lady BUG Trail" to discover more truth about a particular subject. I encourage you to take as many Lady BUG Trails as you want! This is similar to the popular "rabbit trail." According to my husband (an engineer in the business world), taking a "rabbit trail" is following a thought process that meanders, is hard to follow, and doesn't necessarily lead back to the main point. (This can be frustrating in a business meeting!) In comparison, the Lady BUG Trail is a thought process that meanders but because you're meandering in God's Word the trail usually leads to a new discovery or "better understanding" which – VOILA! – is the purpose of this study. Every single word, phrase, and paragraph in God's Word is useful to us! (2 Timothy 3:16-17) In our pilot study, some Lady BUG Sisters said that many of their fondest "Aha!" moments with God happened while strolling down a Lady

BUG Trail. You may want to use your own Bible's index and concordance or invest in an exhaustive concordance. There are also many wonderful Bible Study tools (commentaries, Bible dictionaries, multiple Bible translations) available FREE on-line. My favorites are www.biblegateway.com and www.heartlight.org. I have these great websites bookmarked and use them every day!

Lady BUG Fast Food Cards

Along the journey, you will come across Scriptures that touch your heart and feed your soul. I'd like you to remember that Truth is Good Food! Write the Scripture on a 3 x 5 note card. Date it and PERSONALIZE it to meet your life's situation. My dear friend, Suzan, came up with an idea to make a "snack pack" to store all of the fast food cards! Try it. You'll like it! Buy a 3x5 note card holder, decorate it with ladybugs and write Truth is Good Food across the front! Take your snack pack with you wherever you go so you will have a nutritious "snack" to sustain you throughout the day! I learned that ladybugs have a "voracious" appetite! The word voracious means "craving or consuming large quantities of food; exceedingly eager." One day I misspelled voracious (spelling it with an e) which prompted a wonderful discovery! The word veracious means "characterized by truthfulness; true, accurate, or honest." Woo Woo! At that moment, I realized God wants us to be like the ladybug, having a voracious appetite for His veracious food (the Word).

No Rules...Just Write!

Throughout the Bible Study you will find the phrase, No Rules...Just Write! This means exactly what it says. You can write whatever you want! There are no wrong answers. Pause, ponder, praise, pontificate. Pour out your heart in prayer. Your way is the right way! Please consider this a Journal for your Journey, not just an ordinary workbook. This journaling is a heart-smart way to become more intimate with God. No two "journals" will look alike. Praise God! God made us all different for a reason. (See 1 Corinthians 12:12-31.) Yet, He has made each of us in His image. When we come together and share our unique thoughts and feelings with each other we all get to see a fuller picture of God! As for sharing, you get to decide if you want to share what you write with the group. That is a personal decision.

Privacy Pledge

If you are using this workbook in a group setting, please do whatever it takes to provide a place of SAFE SHARING. I encourage each group member to make a privacy pledge to every other member of the group, "What you say here, stays here!" Hear my heart on this one, STICK TO IT! Confidentiality is crucial and an essential element in sincere Lady BUG Sisterhood!

Living the Lyrics

Ephesians 5:19-20 tells us to "speak to one another with psalms, hymns, and spiritual songs." During this Bible Study we are going to sing many songs – some familiar and some brand new. I want us to learn the lyrics and love the lyrics. But, above all, I want us to LIVE THE LYRICS in our daily lives. This entails analyzing what we are actually singing and, in some cases, defining archaic language or studying the "rest of the story" about how the song was born.

Becoming Berean BUGs: Read Acts 17:10-12

Do you want to become a noble Berean BUG? I do! Let's follow in the Bereans' footsteps by adopting this motto for our journey. **"Berean BUGs Eagerly Examine Every Day!"** In addition, please add "to see if what Denell says is true!" I am in NO WAY equating myself with Paul, except to say as author of this Bible Study I want to speak the truth! But, please don't ever take my word for it! Examine for yourselves daily! In our pilot study, we purchased a magnifying glass for each Sister and encouraged her to use it on her daily discovery walks with God. You might want to get your own magnifying glass and label it with a ladybug sticker and Acts 17:11. One more thought. **"Embrace Each Epiphany!"** By definition, the word embrace means "to clasp or hold; to take in with the eyes or mind; to accept eagerly!" An epiphany is "a spiritual event in which the essence of a given object of manifestation appears to the subject, as in a sudden flash of recognition." In other words, when you have an "Aha!" moment accept it eagerly and hold on to it! This will often be the Holy Spirit nudging you with discernment. What a treasure!

Lost in Translation?

There are many wonderful translations of the Bible. You are welcome to use any version you prefer for your personal study. However, this Bible Study was primarily written using the ***New International Version.*** Please keep this version handy for times when I ask you to find a particular phrase or to fill in blanks with specific words.

Introduction

LADYBUGS. Petite, popular, polka-dotted and particularly precious! Children adore them. Gardeners rely on them. What's not to love? When my sister-in-law, Carol, handed me a folder back in December of 2003, I immediately thought, "What a unique idea!" Carol had attended a ladies retreat a few months before in Alabama. Knowing that I was a ladies retreat speaker, she gave me this folder to add to my repertoire of ideas. The folder was orange with a piece of green construction paper glued to the front. (Thank you, Elizabeth Staten from Alabama, for the original folder design!) Flying across the folder was a red ladybug with black spots, created with a die cut machine. The following words were printed on the folder:

Ladies
B etter
U nderstanding
G od

Being a lover of acronyms, the idea grabbed my attention. My mind began to dance with images of ladybug nametags, decorations, etc. I had previously spoken about The Friendship Garden, so naturally, I felt that these cute little creatures would be added to the friendship lessons (perhaps they could become the mascot of our garden!).

Picture this: a 39-year-old woman, squeezed into a child-size chair in the children's section of Barnes & Noble, poring over every ladybug book in the store, wildly taking notes like there's no tomorrow. "*God, do you actually want me to learn about ladybugs? If so, what do you want me to know about these little creatures?*" As I surfed the Internet printing off page after page of ladybug fun facts, I asked, "*God, how are these facts going to be helpful at all? What do you want me to do with all of this information? How will this glorify you?*" Months pass. Imagine a now-40-year-old woman, on her hands and knees in the local garden center with a magnifying glass observing the habits of ladybugs; looking for aphids; sprinkling "dew" on the roses; taking photographs. "*God, please help me! I've gone ladybug crazy! What does all of this mean? How could this possibly have anything to do with better understanding YOU? Ladybugs are not even mentioned in the Bible!*"

Little did I know that God had a purpose in mind for these ladybugs and for ME! (See Proverbs 19:21.) For the past three years God has used these ladybugs to show His TRUTH to me in more creative ways than I can wrap my mind around. As I started digging in the Word, I heard a wee voice calling from within whispering, EAT MY WORDS! THEY'RE IN YOUR BIBLE! This was so amazing because it happened over and over again! EAT MY WORDS! THEY'RE IN YOUR BIBLE! The more I "ate His words" the hungrier I became! One day I came across this scripture. **Proverbs 6:6-11.** Fill in these blanks from verse 6 in the NIV Bible. ________to the ________, you sluggard; consider its ways and be ________________!

This passage really spoke to my heart. I thought it was waaaaaaay cool that the proverbial writer suggests that we can learn valuable life lessons simply by observing the way an insect behaves. According to this verse, there are three steps: Go, Consider its ways, Be wise!

At that moment, I felt like God was giving me a formula for the ladybugs, too! Go to the ladybug, Denell. Consider her ways. Be wise! Through many hours of Bible study and prayer God spoke volumes to my heart. God, through the ladybugs, taught me the NECESSITY of coming to the garden alone while the dew is still on the roses. **B**etter **U**nderstanding **G**od became my daily objective. Devouring His Word became my daily delight! In the course of time, as I spoke about the Lady BUGs at ladies retreats and other events, people began to give me Lady BUG gifts. You name it, I've received it! Some even started referring to me as the Lady BUG Lady.

Then...one ordinary day, I received an e-mail from a dear friend who wanted my assistance making some ladybug nametags for an upcoming seminar called **Free To Go**. I was thrilled to find out that the seminar speakers also had a passion for ladybugs! They requested a ladybug "in flight" to be placed on the nametags & magnets. I agreed to make the materials and they invited me to attend the seminar. "What's FREE TO GO about?" I asked. They told me it would be about Healing The Child Within...teaching me (and "my little girl within") how to be FREE TO GO in this life! To my surprise, my insides became a little wobbly. To be perfectly honest, I was having some **angst** about attending a seminar entitled Free To Go. Perhaps, my Big Girl and my Little Girl were having a bit of a struggle about how this might change "our" life? Sometimes, my ponderings turn into poetry. This is the poem I wrote that day.

Voices & Choices

You're free to go
She heard the voice say
But her Big Girl heart
Implored her to stay
In the prison of comfort
Called Status Quo
With her cell mates (her soul mates)
What If & Don't Know
Go where?
Asked her fear of unknown places
Go with whom?
Asked her caution of unknown faces
Free to go anywhere with GOD
Said the voice
Then, her Little Girl heart whispered
Wow...what a choice!

It seems to me that life, in a nutshell, is all about Voices and Choices! I chose to be BRAVE and attend the Free To Go seminar and ladies, let me just say, my life will never be the same! Shortly after that seminar, God opened the door wide for me to write and teach this Bible study (the one you are reading now). I wish I could tell you that I flew right through that door with my new Free to Go wings of FAITH! But, the more accurate answer would be this: I had a Moses Moment. ***"****Who am I, Lord, to actually write a Bible Study? I've written a few poems and a few songs, Lord, but...write the whole curriculum? Who ME?****"*** This feeling of "angst" prompted me to dig in God's Word for some food for thought from MOSES. His story took my breath away!!! His story changed my life. His story reinforced the idea even MORE that our life is all determined by Voices and Choices!I am reminded of the chorus of that great song Voice of Truth:

The voice of Truth tells me a different story
The voice of Truth says, "Do not be afraid!"
And the voice of Truth says, "This is for My glory"
Out of all the voices calling out to me
I will choose to listen and believe the voice of truth!

Lady BUG Sisters, if you want to make one commitment that will incredibly and enormously transform your life, do this: CHOOSE to LISTEN and BELIEVE the voice of Truth! If you are truly committed, write your commitment below, sign and date it.

____

____

____

Date________________ Signature____________________________

In our Week One "homework" time together I want to share some Moses Moments with you. Won't you join me in the garden? Pull up a leaf and stay a while. I've saved a "SPOT" just for you!

Chapter 1:

When God Says GO, Do I Say Whoa?

Day 1: Ready, Set, Go

Snack to nibble on: Exodus 3:10 So now, GO. I am sending you to Pharaoh to bring my people the Israelites out of Egypt.

Read Exodus 3:1-12 in the NIV Bible.

According to "scriptural math" Moses was about 80 years old when God called to him from within the bush. (Math lovers see Acts 7:23 plus Acts 7:30 = Mo's age!)

What was Moses busy doing when he saw the strange sight? (v. 1)

___

Hmmm...who else do we know in Holy Writ that was called to do God's work while "tending" the flock? (See 1 Samuel 16:10-12 and 2 Samuel 7:8.)

___

God, in His infinite wisdom, called Moses and David to "shepherd" God's people while they were smack dab in the middle of tending sheep! No co-inky-dink there! Notice what **Psalm 78:70-72** says about David. (We could spend all day discussing how David "shepherded" with integrity of heart, but that's a story for another day!)

How did the angel of the Lord appear to Moses? (See Exodus 3:2)

___

Read verse 4 carefully. **When** did God actually call to Moses?

___

I'm intrigued that the LORD saw Moses had "gone over to look" at the bush. Consider verse 3 from the Amplified version of the Bible:

And Moses said, I will now ***turn aside*** *and see this great sight, why the bush is not burned. (Exodus 3:3 AMP)*

Was Moses talking to the sheep or to himself? I have a feeling he was talking to himself. (My dad often says, "Then, I said to myself, Self....") ☺ This is a lesson for us. Maybe in our own lives there's been a fiery bush nearby. Perhaps God was waiting and watching from the flames to see if we would ***turn aside*** and see the great sight! Have we been too busy "tending" to "turn" and approach the flames? Honestly explore this concept with an example from your own life. If you can't think of an example from your past...Ahhh....then consider the future! No Rules...Just WRITE!

____

____

____

When God called to Moses from within the bush, how did Moses respond? (Exodus 3:4)

____

Now, read Isaiah 6:8. God asked two very important questions. What were they?

1. ______________________________________

2. ______________________________________

Notice that God is making a distinction. HE will do the ***sending***. He wants to know who will do the ***going.***

How did Isaiah respond? (Isaiah 6:8)

____

Wouldn't it be grand if our friend Moses had uttered these words? (But, then again, he wouldn't have learned a valuable lesson, so let's continue on and find out what he learned!) Read **Exodus 3:4-6.** Immediately after Moses says, "Here I am" God says, "Do not come any closer...take off your sandals, for the place where you are standing is holy ground." Let's take a Lady BUG trail down Barefoot Lane.

In 1995, our family lived on the island of Kyushu, Japan for three months. One of the customs we had to get "accustomed" to was always removing our shoes before entering a building, restaurant, and even our apartment. To enter our apartment we had to go through two doors. The first door led to an entryway, called the *genkan*. This was the place where we removed our outside shoes and parked them in the *getabako*, a shoe cupboard. We would then put on our house slippers and enter the second door, taking a step up into our apartment. For the first few weeks, this custom was somewhat fun. I remember the day, however, when the custom got OLD. I was tired of tofu, sick of sushi, and fed up with being a foreigner! I was up to my eyeballs with Konnichiwa and was pouting about sleeping on a bed that smelled like grass. I vividly remember walking straight through the entryway and into my apartment STOMPING around with my dirty tennis shoes on mumbling, "I can wear my outside shoes inside if I want to!" (Yes, I was a basket case that day which is probably why I'm so drawn to Moses! Ha.)

A survey was taken as to why the Japanese have the custom of removing their shoes. [1] The responses are interesting:

For the sake of cleanliness
Because they want to relax
To draw the line between inside and outside (private & public)
To directly feel the floor with their feet

I wonder. What were God's main reasons for asking Moses to remove his shoes? What does His request say to your heart?

____

____

Perhaps there were many reasons. I wonder if God wanted Moses to "draw the line between inside and outside." God specifically told Moses that he was standing on "holy ground." Maybe God wanted Moses to directly feel that "holy ground" with his bare feet! He didn't want anything coming between them. Whatever the reasons, I am sure that Moses got those sandals off as fast as he could!

Let's look back at our passage in Exodus 3:5-6. Moses has just stated, "Here I am." Now, God proceeds to get to the bottom line with, "This is Who I am!" Did you notice how precise He was? Fill in the blanks from verse 6.

Then he said, "I am the God of your __________, the God of __________, the God of __________ and the God of __________."

According to verse 6, why did Moses hide his face?

____

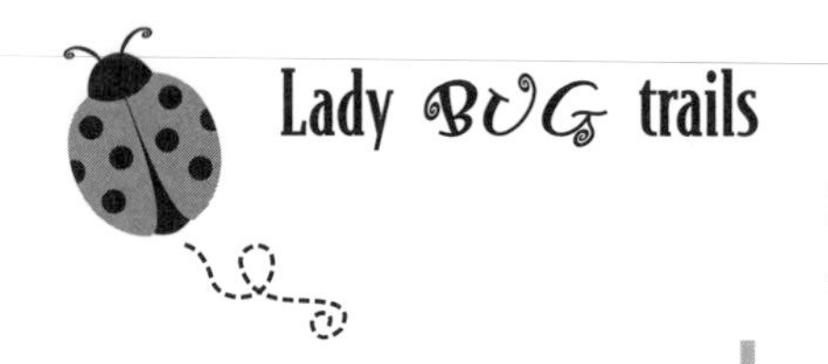

Read **Exodus 3:7-10 using the NIV Bible.** Also, take a quick glance at Exodus 2:25. If you write in your Bible (it's ok, I promise!) please circle the 9-letter word that begins with a c. Now, write that same word in big, bold letters below and add an exclamation mark for emphasis!

____

When God saw the misery of His people and heard them crying out, He was concerned! You might laugh out loud (as I did) to find out that the original Hebrew word for "concerned" in this context is **yada.** I know in today's culture we use "yada yada" in a different way. I asked my seven-year-old daughter, Alli, what yada yada means and she said, "You know, Mom, it means blah, blah, blah!"

Well, this is NOT the case in the account of Moses. The Hebrew term **yada** actually means "to know, to learn, to perceive, recognize, and understand." [2] I find comfort in the truth that God knows, recognizes, and understands our misery! Do you also find comfort in this truth? Explain.

____

____

In verse 8 God tells Moses that He has a 2-part plan. He will **rescue** the Israelites from the hand of the Egyptians. He will bring them up out of that land into a good and spacious land, a land flowing with milk and honey.

Moses, likely, was relieved to know that God was going to rescue His people even though he, himself, had botched the job 40 years ago.

Let's do a little mind reading in **Acts 7:23-29.** Luke, the inspired writer, tells us that Moses, age 40, saw an Israelite being mistreated by an Egyptian. Moses "went to his defense" (or, swooped in to save the day!) by killing the Egyptian. Moses to the Rescue! Woo-Hoo! However, things didn't quite go the way he had hoped. In verse 25 we actually get to read his thoughts. According to Acts 7:25, what did Moses think his own people would realize?

____

____

This must have been quite a blow to Ole MO! Flip back to Exodus 2:15 and notice that upon hearing the news, Pharaoh tried to kill him so he FLED (which literally means escaped, eluded & ran away) to Midian. [3]

Here's a little jewel worth examining. Use your magnifying glass to get a closer look. Exodus 2:15-17. Fill in the blanks from verse 17. (NIV Bible)

Some shepherds came along and drove them away, but Moses got up and ____ __ ______ ________ and watered their flock.

Moses was still on the run from his previous "heroic" deed and apparently was still wearing his Prince of Egypt Super Hero cape! Fast forward 40 years and let's join Moses where we left him at the bush. God has just told Moses that He has "come down" to "rescue" His people. Moses must be feeling pretty perky about the plan! But, then in verse 10, the PLAN hits the FAN!

Write Exodus 3:10. (NIV Bible)

____

____

Circle the 2-letter word that begins with a g. In fact, if you have a red pen, circle that word in RED and make a red light out of it!!!! This seems a little odd. GO is a green light, right? Well, in Moses' situation, that little word GO stopped him in his tracks. Close your eyes. Grab a dry-erase marker and sketch the scene on the whiteboard in your mind. God is saying, "So now, **GO**. I am **sending** YOU." Do you see the look on that ole' shepherd's face? Imagine what may have been going through his mind. Record your first thoughts here.

____

____

Did Moses pull out the Unworthy laundry list? Did he remember why he had fled for his life in the first place? Did he hear the voices of the past sneering, "Who made you ruler and judge over us?" (Exodus 2:14) Did he say to himself, "Who me? But, I've been put out to pasture for 40 years! Me, to the rescue? I've been there. Done that. Bought the tunic! I turned in my Super Hero cape years ago!" I wonder if Moses really understood what God was asking. Did he hear the words "I am sending you" and think that God was expecting him to go forth and rescue? Did he not fully realize, yet, that it is God and God, alone, who can truly Rescue?!

How about you? Have you seen a common bush on fire lately? Has something happened in your ordinary day that seemed a bit extraordinary and you wondered, "Could that be God?" Or, have you been zooming through life in the fast lane, too busy to see anything but the next item on the to-do list?

____

____

Take some time to Stop, Look, and Listen. Turn aside from the ordinary to gaze upon the extraordinary! What is your response when you hear God say Go? Is there a red light or a green light in your heart? Remember, it is God who does the "sending" if we're not too busy "tending." For now, I will leave you to ponder this profound poetic piece by one of my all-time favorite poets. May we open our eyes, take off our shoes, gaze into the flames and look fr HIM!

Earth's crammed with heaven,
And every common bush afire with God;
But only he who sees, takes off his shoes -
The rest sit round it and pluck blackberries.

-Elizabeth Barrett Browning

What is ONE THING you better understand about God? Tell Him as you pour out your heart in prayer!

____

____

____

____

____

____

Day 2: Living The Lyrics: If You Say Go

We're about to make some rather bold declarations to God! Before singing the song, read the lyrics. Do you agree with what you will be singing? Internalize the truth you find. Then, sing the song.

If You Say Go

(Words & Music by Diane Thiel)

If You say go, we will go
If You say wait, we will wait
If You say step out on the water
And they say it can't be done
We'll fix our eyes on You
And we will come!
(Repeat)

Chorus:
Your ways are higher than our ways
And the plans that You have made
Are good and true
If you call us to the fire
You will not withdraw Your hand
We'll gaze into the flames
And look for You

We'll fix our eyes on You and we will come!

Allow these scriptures to speak to your heart. Jot down nuggets of truth. Highlight the "food" for thought that is most nourishing to you!

GO:

Exodus 3:10, 16, 18; 4:12

For a waaaaaay cool example of **"going & waiting"** see Exodus 40:34-38.

WAIT:

Psalm 5:3

Psalm 27:14

Psalm 130:5

Isaiah 30:18

Psalm 40:1

Hebrews 9:28

STEP OUT ON THE WATER/COME:

Matthew 14:28-29

FIX OUR EYES:

Hebrews 12:2

Proverbs 4:25

2 Corinthians 4:18

YOUR WAYS ARE HIGHER:

Isaiah 55:9

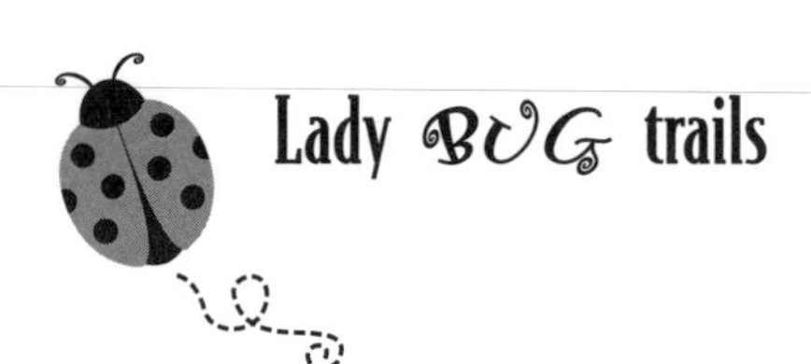

PLANS:

Psalm 33:11

Proverbs 19:21

Jeremiah 29:11

GAZE INTO THE FLAMES:

Exodus 3:2; Acts 7:30

Isaiah 43:2

Daniel 3:8-30

Close in prayer expressing how you will choose to LIVE THE LYRICS of this great song this week!

Dear God, when you say go I will...

Day 3: Who Am I?

Snack to nibble on: Exodus 3:11 But Moses said to God, "Who am I, that I should go to Pharaoh and bring the Israelites out of Egypt?"

Refresh the story in your mind by reading Exodus 3:1-12.

Now, get ready for my favorite part of the story! In verse 10 God uses some emphatic words. (Words that sometimes – let's face it - are not our favorite words!)

Now (not later, or at a more convenient time, ready or not, here you go!)
GO (a verb of action; as opposed to umm...stalling, stammering, stopping!)
I am (whoa...no miscommunication as to Who is doing the sending)
Sending (the Hebrew word for send is *salah* "to send out; to be sent away; to let go; to release")
YOU (not his father-in-law, not some other young whippersnapper with "skills")

In your opinion, which of those 5 words gave Moses the most cause for pause? Why?

____

____

Chew on verse 11. Moses asks the question, "Who am I, that I should GO...?" How many times in my own life have I asked this same question, "Who am I, Lord, that I should..." (Fill in the blanks with a million things.) Does his question speak to your heart? Perhaps you're having your own "Who am I?" moment this week. Do you smell "smoke" and wonder where the "fire" is? Stop, Drop & Pray! Clarity is just a breath away. Ask God, "Who am I?" Record what He reveals to you.

____

____

____

In Exodus 3:12 we find God's answer to Moses. There are two parts to it.

I will be with you!
I will even give a sign to you!

What part of God's answer prompts you to don your thinking cap?

____

____

Lady BUG trails

Here are my thoughts. Where's the answer to Mo's question? Didn't he ask, "Who am I?" Where's the part where God tells Moses who he is? Where's the part where God doles out "warm fuzzies" and compliments? Where's the part where He reminds Moses of how "qualified" he really is? This could be a case in point for the bumper sticker stating, **God does not call the qualified, He qualifies the called!** Take out your magnifying glass and examine verse 12 carefully. Allow me to paraphrase God's answer to Moses.

Moses, this rescue mission is not about you. I haven't chosen you because of what you've done. I haven't chosen you because of who you are. This mission is about Who I am! ***I will be with you.*** *What more could you possibly need? Were you listening when I told you that I would be the Rescuer here? No need to dust off the Super Hero cape. I'll take you just as you are, barefoot and desert-worn. I am sending you. I want you to GO! And,* ***when*** *you have brought My people out of Egypt, you will worship Me on this mountain.*

I love the way God put things in perspective. Unfortunately, Moses was still suffering from cold feet. (Perhaps he should have moved a little closer to the flames to warm his tootsies!) It seems to me that Moses still didn't "get the picture." Imagine hearing Almighty God's voice saying, "I will be with you!" Would that remove all fear and doubt or, would the comfort zone still be too...well, comfy!

Surely he'd heard Abraham's story.

> Genesis 26:3 Stay in this land for a while, and ***I will be with you*** and will bless you. For to you and your descendants I will give all these lands and will confirm the oath I swore to your father Abraham.

Surely he'd heard Isaac's story.

> Genesis 26:24 That night the LORD appeared to Isaac and said, "I am the God of your father Abraham. Do not be afraid, for ***I am with you***; I will bless you and will increase the number of your descendants for the sake of my servant Abraham."

Surely he'd heard Jacob's story.

> Genesis 28:15 ***I am with you*** and will watch over you wherever you go, and I will bring you back to this land. ***I will not leave you until I have done what I have promised you."***

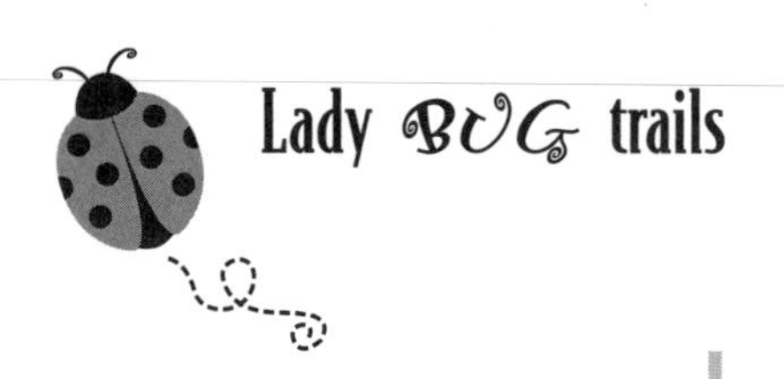

I'm wondering if God was jogging Mo's memory, reminding him of His faithfulness to his forefathers. Hmmm...this situation sounds all-too familiar! Do we do the same thing today? When God calls us to GO, do we say, "Whoa?!" Do we answer His voice from the fiery flame with reluctant excuses that are rather lame? If, by chance, you've ever given God a lame excuse, record one or two here.

But, Who am I? I'm a nobody. Why are you choosing me? I'm not up to the task. What's up with that? Haven't we heard the stories of our forefathers? We have far MORE history than Moses did to prove that God means what He says when He utters the words **I will be with you**! Let's take a stroll down Bible Land Lane and listen to the voice of God.

What did God tell Joshua?

> Joshua 1:5 No one will be able to stand up against you all the days of your life. ***As I was with Moses, so I will be with you; I will never leave you nor forsake you.***

What did God tell Gideon?

> Judges 6:14 The LORD turned to Gideon and said, "Go in the strength you have and save Israel out of Midian's hand. ***Am I not sending you?***" 15 "But Lord," Gideon asked, "How can I save Israel? My clan is the weakest in Manasseh, and I am the least in my family." 16 The LORD answered, "***I will be with you***, and you will strike down all the Midianites together." (Did you notice Gideon's Who Am I moment in verse 15?)

What did David know about God?

> Psalm 118:6 ***The LORD is with me***; I will not be afraid. What can man do to me?
> Psalm 118:7 ***The LORD is with me***; he is my helper. I will look in triumph on my enemies.

What did God tell Jeremiah? Pay close attention to verses 8 and 19. Who comes to the rescue? ☺

> Jeremiah 1:7 But the LORD said to me, "Do not say, 'I am only a child.' You must go to everyone I send you to and say whatever I command you. 8 Do not be afraid of them, for ***I am with you and will rescue you***," declares the LORD.

Jeremiah 1:19 They will fight against you but will not overcome you, for ***I am with you and will rescue you,*** " declares the LORD.

Remember what God promised Isaiah.

Isaiah 41:10 So do not fear, for ***I am with you;***
do not be dismayed, for I am your God.
I will strengthen you and help you;
I will uphold you with my righteous right hand.

Isaiah 43:2 When you pass through the waters,
I will be with you;
and when you pass through the rivers,
they will not sweep over you.
When you walk through the fire,
you will not be burned;
the flames will not set you ablaze.

Surely we've heard what the Lord said to Paul.

Acts 18:9 One night the Lord spoke to Paul in a vision: "Do not be afraid; keep on speaking, do not be silent. 10 For ***I am with you,*** and no one is going to attack and harm you, because I have many people in this city." 11 So Paul stayed for a year and a half, teaching them the word of God.

Read Matthew 28:16-20. Then read John 14:15-21.

Spend a few minutes with your eyes closed and your heart open. Allow these truths to sink in. DEEP. Do these passages speak a specific message to your specific circumstances? If so, write away!!!!!

Day 4: Living The Lyrics: Who Am I?

On those days I choose to overwhelm myself with the question "Who Am I?", I pray that I will choose to overwhelm myself even MORE with God's comforting promise, "As I was with Moses, I am with you!" I'll choose to listen to God's voice saying, "I will never leave you, I will never forsake you. I will not leave you until I have done what I have promised you."

Who Am I?

(lyrics by Mark Hall)

Who am I, that the Lord of all the earth
Would care to know my name
Would care to feel my hurt
Who am I, that the Bright and Morning Star
Would choose to light the way
For my ever wandering heart

CHORUS:
Not because of who I am
But because of what You've done
Not because of what I've done
But because of Who You are

I am a flower quickly fading
Here today and gone tomorrow
A wave tossed in the ocean
A vapor in the wind
Still You hear me when I'm calling
Lord, You catch me when I'm falling
And You've told me who I am
I am Yours, I am Yours

Who am I, that the eyes that see my sin
Would look on me with love and watch me rise again
Who am I, that the voice that calmed the sea
Would call out through the rain
And calm the storm in me

How does that song speak to your heart?

Read the following passages and write a phrase from the song that this scripture confirms. Then, take it one step further and write how you can apply this particular phrase to your own life! Enjoy digging deep. Find pleasure in the pondering.

Exodus 3:11

Exodus 33:17

1 Samuel 18:18

Psalm 27:1

Psalm 107:29

Psalm 119:93-94

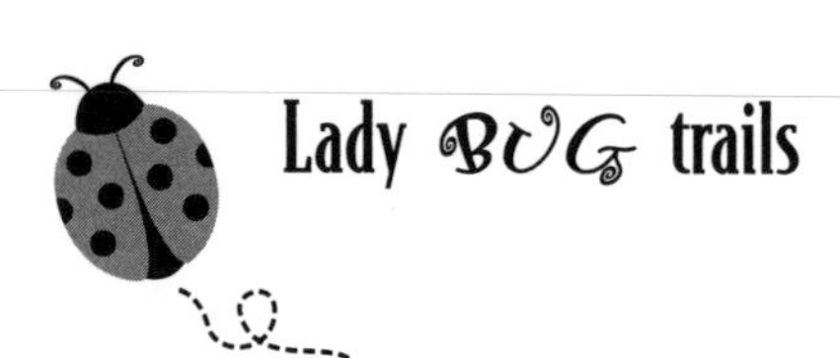

Isaiah 43:1

Matthew 8:26

James 1:6, 10

Revelation 22:16

For a special treat, read **Psalm 139**. Join David in praising God for fearfully and wonderfully making you!

Finally, commit to LIVING THESE LYRICS all day long! Grab a wooden spoon and belt out the chorus while cooking dinner. Sing it at the top of your lungs in the shower. Pray these words before going to sleep tonight and whisper to God, "I am so glad I am Yours!"

[1] Japanese Culture and Daily Life
[2] Baker
[3] Goodrick

Chapter 2:

When God Says GO,
Do I Say NO?

Day 1: Suppose...

Lady BUG trails

Snack to nibble on: Exodus 3:13 Moses said to God, "Suppose I go...and they ask me, 'What is his name?' Then what shall I tell them?"

Read Exodus 3:13-22.

Suppose. According to our modern dictionary, suppose means "to assume (something) to be true or real for the sake of an argument or explanation." [1] The original Hebrew word for suppose is ***hinneh***, which is "an interjection meaning behold, look, now, or if. It is used to express strong feelings." [2]

I will confess to you that the first thing I did when I read verse 13 was laugh out loud in commiserating fashion. *I'm there with ya, Moses! I suffer from "Suppose I Go Syndrome", too! Suppose I go teach a Bible class and the ladies start asking questions. Suppose I don't have the answers? Suppose they want to know intimate details about God...things that remain a mystery to me...what shall I tell them?*

Have you ever suffered from "Suppose I Go Syndrome"? If so, what were your thoughts and feelings?

____

____

____

____

____

____

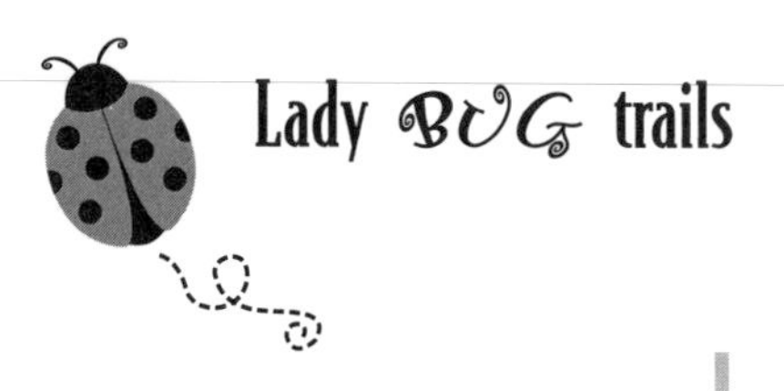

Sometimes, fear of the unknown prompts us to conjure up Suppose Scenarios. We want to cover all of our bases and devise plan A, B, and C. Before an interview the person being interviewed usually requests a copy of the questions so that he/she will have time to plan their responses. It's intriguing that Moses was acting this out on the stage in his mind. He already knew what he would tell the Israelites, "The God of your fathers has sent me to you."

Let's rewind our minds to how God introduced Himself to Moses right after he shed his sandals. Look at Exodus 3:6. "I am the God of your father, the God of Abraham, the God of Isaac and the God of Jacob." This declaration caused Moses to hide his face, out of sheer fear! So, why then, would Moses suppose that this would not be "good enough" for the Israelites? Why would they want to know His name? (v. 13)

Record your thoughts here.

____

____

____

____

____

____

I took a Lady BUG trail down Bible Names Lane and found several fun facts in the *Holman Bible Dictionary*. To the ancient world, a person's name expressed "essence." To know the name of a person was to know that person's total character and nature. The name of God revealed His relationship with His people. His name is known only when He chooses to make it known! Before Moses' encounter with God in the Midianite desert, God was known generally as the "God of the Fathers." [3]

Take a peek at Exodus 6:3. (Yes, we're fast forwarding into the future for a reason! Isn't it fun to have the luxury of knowing the whole story?)

Write Exodus 6:3.

____

____

____

____

____

By what name did God appear to Abraham, Isaac, and Jacob?

____

____

Lady BUG trails

The Hebrew name for God Almighty is "El Shaddai." (Feel free to hum Amy Grant's "El Shaddai" song throughout the rest of the day!)

God specifically says that He did **NOT** make Himself known to them by what name? ______________________________

I especially love the way the Amplified Bible states this verse.

> Exodus 6:3 (AMP) I appeared to Abraham, to Isaac, and to Jacob as God Almighty [El-Shaddai], but by My name the Lord [**Yahweh**—the redemptive name of God] I did not make Myself known to them [in acts and great miracles].

Yahweh is the English pronunciation of the Hebrew consonants YHWH.[4] (The written Hebrew language excluded vowels.) The NIV version and other versions translate this word as LORD (in all caps). When God told Moses "I am who I am...tell them I AM has sent me to you" (Exodus 3:14) God was introducing Himself INTIMATELY to Moses, divulging His "personal" name and sharing His very essence with him.

What does "I am who I am" mean to you?

____

____

____

____

Read Exodus 33:11. How did Yahweh speak to Moses?

____

____

____

____

Face-to-face! Now, that's intimacy! Yahweh is used more than 6,000 times throughout the Old Testament. Shazam!

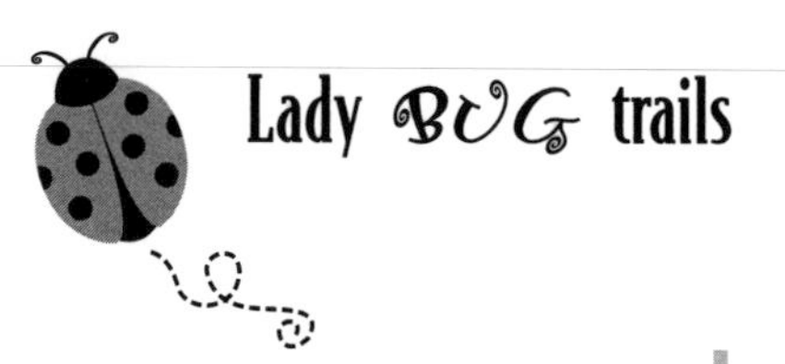

Study this definition of Yahweh, "the proper name of the one true God; knowledge and use of the name implies personal or covenant relationship; the name pictures God as the one who exists and/or causes existence." [5] Now, let's put ourselves in Moses' shoes (or rather, in his bare feet). Go back to Exodus 3:15 and read the verse intently. What thoughts or feelings might be bubbling forth?

____

____

____

____

____

____

It's interesting that God doesn't just answer the question by giving Moses His Name. He then proceeds to tell him, in great detail, exactly what will happen. Allow me to summarize verses 16-22. God tells Moses to:

GO! (There's that 2-letter, power-packed word again.)
Assemble Israel's elders, tell them my Name and my promise.
They will listen!
GO with the elders to Egypt's king, tell him my Name, and ask to take a 3-day journey to offer sacrifices.
The king will say NO.
I will perform wonders.
After that, he <u>will</u> let you GO.
I will also make sure the Egyptians are willing to give silver, gold, and clothing to the Israelites, which means you will plunder the Egyptians!

Talk about crystal ball clarity! God said it all! He had the itinerary planned to the Nth degree. Wouldn't it be grand to know the "plan" this intimately? Or would it be? What is your opinion? No Rules...Just Write!

____

____

____

____

____

____

____

What does God's Word have to say about **plans**? Let's take a Lady BUG trail down Plans Lane and see what we can find out!

Psalm 33:11 ____

____

Proverbs 19:21 ____

____

Jeremiah 29:11 ____

____

Moses got even more than what he asked for! He asked for a name and got the entire game plan. Hmmm...one would think with this kind of Blessed Assurance that Moses would have jumped right on the band wagon. He DID NOT!

How about you? Are you dealing with a little bit of "Suppose I Go Syndrome", too? Is fear of the unknown crouching at your door? Are you busy devising Plan A, Plan B, and Plan C forgetting that the only plan that really counts - the only plan that actually matters - is **Plan G?** (God's plan.)

____

____

____

What is one thing you better understand about God today?

____

____

____

Offer a prayer of thanksgiving that the PLANS are in God's hands! Commit your whole heart to trusting in His timetable.

____

____

____

____

____

Day 2: A Poem to Ponder: Who I Am

Let's spend some time together considering a poem that speaks to the heart of Better Understanding God and who He is!

Who I Am

While praying one day
a woman asked,
"Who are You, Lord?"
He answered, "I AM."
"But who is, I AM?" she asked.
And He replied, "I Am Love, I Am Peace,
I Am Grace, I Am Joy,
I Am the Way, the Truth, and the Light,
I Am the Comforter, I Am Strength, I Am Safety,
I Am Shelter, I Am Power, I Am the Creator,
I Am the Beginning and the End
I Am the Most High."
The woman with tears in her eyes
looked toward heaven and said,
"Now I understand. But, Lord, Who am I?"
Then God tenderly wiped the tears
from her eyes and whispered,
"You are Mine!"

(Author Unknown)

After reading this poem, dig in the Word for at least one scripture that describes each attribute of God. Use the concordance in the back of your Bible or any other "study help" you want. Enjoy the treasure hunt and don't forget to thank God for the jewels you find!

God is Love.

God is Peace.

God is Grace.

God is Joy.

God is the Way, the Truth, and the Light.

God is the Comforter.

God is Strength.

God is Safety.

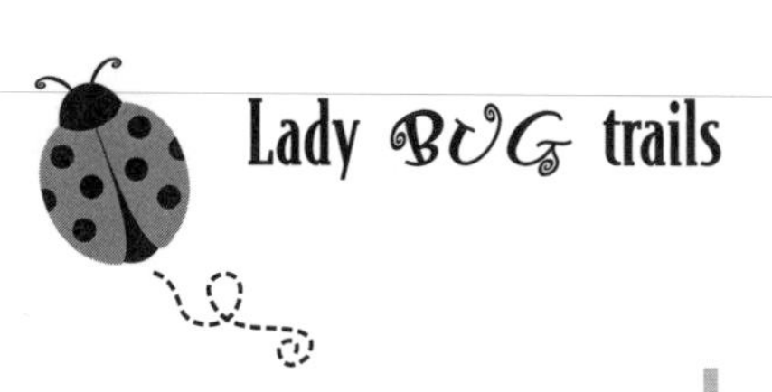

God is Shelter.

God is Power.

God is the Creator.

God is the Beginning and the End.

God is the Most High.

Which attribute of God gives you the most comfort today? Why?

____

____

____

____

____

____

Read Isaiah 43:1 and hear God whisper that same message in your ear! What is your heart's response?

____

____

____

____

Day 3: What If and I've Never

Snack to nibble on: Exodus 4:1, 10 "What if they do not believe me or listen to me...?"; "O Lord, I have never been eloquent...."

Read Exodus 4:1-9.

When I teach 3-year-olds, sometimes they have a little trouble listening with both ears. (Can you imagine?) So, I stop the lesson or activity and proclaim, "Ok, class, TUNE YOUR EARS!" It's hilarious to watch them reach up and "adjust" their hearing. The little girls will often tuck strands of hair behind their ears. The boys will make mechanical noises while rotating their ears like knobs, turning up the volume. (One night, a precious child dramatically announced, "Oops! I can't tune my ears because I left my ears at home!")

Verse 1 of our text today makes me wonder if Moses needed to TUNE HIS EARS! "What if they don't believe me? What if they don't listen to me?" Let's refresh our memories. What had God just told Moses in Exodus 3:18?

___

___

So, what's up with that? I wonder. God had just told Moses that the elders of Israel would listen to him. Now, Moses asks, "What if they don't listen?" This causes me to wonder if Moses was the one with the listening issue! Or, maybe he heard what God said but wanted clarification. Who are THEY anyway? Who's Moses worried about? Did he think God was mistaken about the elders? Was he referring to the Israelites in general? What do you think?

___

___

Theologians and commentators speculate (and many of them disagree) about Moses' motivation for asking this question. You read the text. What does it say to YOU? Describe in your own words what Moses may have been thinking when he asked the question, "What if they do not believe me or listen to me and say, 'The LORD did not appear to you'?"

___

___

___

Put your pen down and sit back in your chair for a moment. Let your mind drift to its thoughtful "spot." Sometimes in my life, I will be reluctant to do or say something because I'm worried about what THEY will think. Or, perhaps I'm fearful of how THEY will react or respond. What if THEY don't believe me? What if THEY don't listen to me? What if THEY misunderstand or misconstrue my message? What if THEY don't accept me? Take some time to consider this. In your own life:

1. Who are THEY? ____

____

2. Do you ever ask "What if THEY..." questions? If so, name a few.

____

____

I love the way God responds to Moses in verse 2. He answers his question by asking a question. Write the question here. Exodus 4:2 (NIV)

____

____

Moses was holding a staff in his hand. The original Hebrew word for staff is ***matteh*** which means "staff, rod, club, a stick used to assist in walking, discipline, and guidance, often highly individualized and used for identification". [6] This staff was certainly "highly individualized" for Moses! Ha. Can you imagine what it was like to watch your staff transformed into a snake right before your very eyes? The text says Moses RAN from it (v. 3). *I'm right there with ya, Moses!* In fact, this story hits a little too close to home and sends chills down my spine. It transports me back in time to my own encounter with a snake.

It's summertime, 1976, not long after my twelfth birthday. I'm living deep in the heart of the piney woods: Hallsville, Texas, population 1,078. It's late in the afternoon, "dusky dark." Mom and I are taking a walk; but not just any walk. We're actually marching! Marching down Galilee Road. (I kid you not!) Mom, with her imaginary piccolo, and I, with my imaginary flute - harmonizing beautifully with trills and vibrato – performing Stars & Stripes Forever for the world. (Mom is the Queen of Impromptu!) All of a sudden, I feel a sting, a sharp sensation that takes my breath away! Looking down, I blink in disbelief! I had marched right on top of a large snake that was now coiling his slithery self around my right ankle. I kick my foot in the air, shaking my leg in a desperate attempt to shake the slimy serpent off! Indeed, he falls off, but not before taking another bite, marking his territory – my ankle – with four fang marks.

*Quick thinking Mom hollers at our neighbor who's hoeing his garden to throw her the hoe so she can chop the snake's head off. She is planning to take the snake's corpse to the hospital with us for identification. The neighbor (we'll call him Mr. McGregor) decides that **he** must be the one to come to the rescue! Instead of handing Mom the hoe over the cyclone fence, he walks ALLLLL the way around it (which was a "fur piece"). In the meantime, a truck comes along and, mistaking my mother's flailing arms for a friendly wave, runs right over the snake! Unfortunately, not a scale on that snake's skin is squished. He slithers off into the woods never to be seen (by us) again! By the time Mr. McGregor to The Rescue arrives on the scene, hoe-in-hand, the snake is long gone!*

As you rightly assume, I did not die from that snakebite. In fact, I was released from the hospital the same day. (Thank you, God!) This story brings back many memories. Some are humorous, but most are NOT. Snakes are scaly and scary. No wonder Moses ran!

With my snake history I am bewildered by what happens in **Exodus 4:4**. Write that verse here.

____

____

Take a snake by the tail? I find it flabbergasting that Moses reached out and took hold of the snake by the tail, seemingly without hesitation, as soon as God told him to do it. According to the NIV Study Bible, throughout much of Egypt's history the pharaoh wore a cobra made of metal on the front of his headdress as a symbol of his sovereignty.[7] Perhaps God was showing Moses that he would be taking another "snake by the tail" soon if he would just agree to GO and let God release His power!

Read Exodus 4:6-9 God performs another miraculous sign by afflicting Moses' skin and then restoring it in a flash. This must have been an enormous eye-opening experience! The other miracle was done with his staff on the ground. This one was performed on his own flesh! Once again, God was outlining for Moses everything he needed. He even offered him Plan A, B, and C!

Plan A – staff becomes snake
Plan B – leprous hand healed
Plan C – Nile River water becomes blood on dry ground

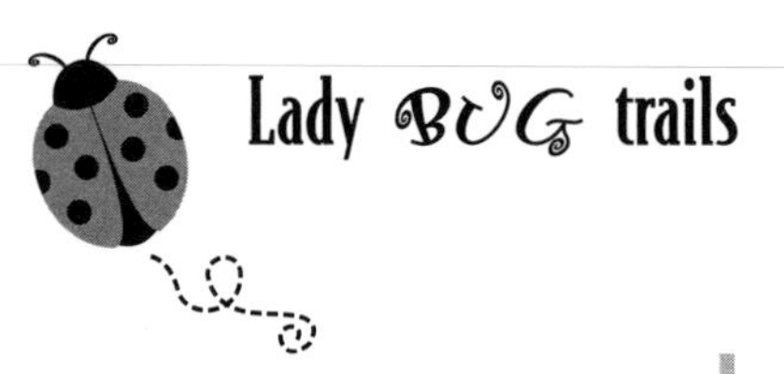

God is pulling out all the stops - equipping, answering questions, offering information, and giving solutions. What more could Moses have wanted? PLENTY! Let's look at **Exodus 4:10**. Write the verse. Then, read it again out loud.

____

____

Do you buy that? I'm having a hard time swallowing that lame excuse. Consider this verse in Acts 7:22. "Moses was educated in all the wisdom of the Egyptians and was **powerful in speech** and action." Hmmm...that doesn't sound too shabby to me! What does Moses tell the LORD about himself in Exodus 6:12 and again in 6:30?

____

This reminds me of Paul! Read 1 Corinthians 2:1-5. In your own words, summarize what Paul was telling the Corinthians.

____

____

I absolutely love what the Lord tells Paul in 2 Corinthians 12:9. "My grace is sufficient for you, for my power is made perfect in weakness!" Paul then concludes that he will boast about his weaknesses so that Christ's power may rest on him. Here's the verse I want to claim for myself. Fill in the blanks from the last sentence of 2 Corinthians 12:10 in huge letters below.

For when I am _______________, then I am __________________!

Lady BUG Sisters, do you believe what you just wrote? This truth can transform our lives dramatically! What "upside down thinking" to delight in weakness! What if we actually give God thanks for our weaknesses? What if we relish the fact that God will use our weakness to display His divine power! Stop and consider how this radical change in thinking could transform your life. Jot down your first thoughts.

____

____

Of course Moses didn't have Paul whispering these great truths in his ear back at the bush. He did, however, have Yahweh, the Great I AM, reassuring him! Let's take a close look at how God answered Moses' "Woe is Me" plea.

Exodus 4:11-12. Once again, the LORD answers his question by asking more questions! Do you hear what I hear? I think God is essentially saying, "Now hear this, Moses! I've told you before and I'll tell you again, this is not about YOU! I'm in charge. I created everything about you. I'm calling the shots. Why do you keep getting hung up on who you are NOT? Take a good look at Who I AM and what I can do!"

Now, here's the most STAGGERING part of the story, in my opinion. Exodus 4:12. In this verse, the LORD says it all and he speaks straight to my own heart!

Now GO!
I will help you speak!
I will teach you what to say!

I'm staring at those promises shouting, "GO, MO, GO!" Here's what I wish. I wish Moses had shouted, "Hallelujah, Thine the Glory, of course I will GO! How could I refuse such a once-in-lifetime deal?" He did NOT. If you've peeked ahead, you already know what his response is to God. We'll cross that bridge tomorrow.

Right now, let's close our time together by asking God to help us internalize what we've learned today. Ask yourself, "What is ONE THING I better understand about God today?" Thank Him for the blessing of that truth!

____

____

____

____

____

____

____

Day 4: Here Am I, Send Someone Else!

Snack to nibble on: Exodus 4:13 But Moses said, "O Lord, please send someone else to do it."

Read Exodus 4:13-17.

Moses chose once again NOT to hop right to it with a resounding *Here am I, send me!* Write verse 13 here.

Now, take a closer look. Breathe in. Breathe out. Slide your feet into Mo's sandals. Hear yourself begging with God, "Pleeeeease send somebody else to do it!"

Have you been there? Felt that? What were the circumstances?

Does Moses sound desperate to you? What's up with that? Explore the emotion behind the eruption. When God said GO, why did MO say NO?

Let's take a few moments to review. God called Moses to do something phenomenal. Instead, he responded with questions and statements revealing his hesitancy.

Who am I?

Suppose I go and they ask, "What is His name?"

What if they do not believe me or listen to me?

Lord, I have never been eloquent...I'm slow of speech and tongue!

Lord, please send someone else to do it!

Which of these questions or statements can you most identify with in your own life? Why?

____

____

This is just my opinion, but I see a progression here.

RELUCTANCE...

RESISTANCE...

REBUTTAL...

REMINDERS...

REBELLION!

What are your thoughts about this progression? Do you agree or disagree? No Rules...Just Write!

____

____

____

____

____

____

Exodus 4:14 says, **"Then the LORD'S anger burned against Moses!"** Take a bite of this food for thought. Chew on it. Ruminate! What was the main reason the LORD'S anger burned against Moses?

____

____

____

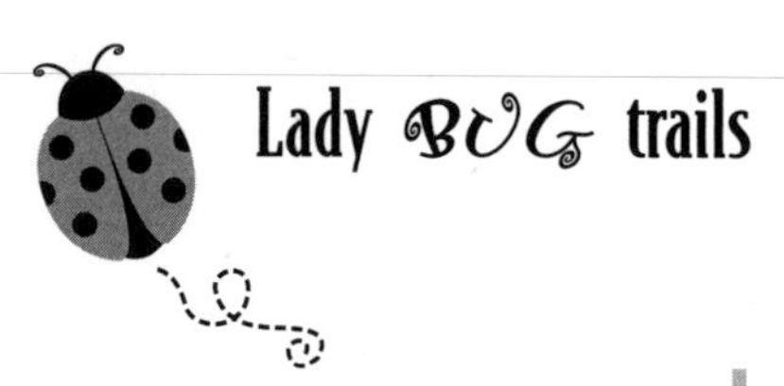

Write Exodus 34:6-7.

Our God is compassionate, gracious, loving, faithful, and forgiving! We can be extremely thankful (as I'm sure Moses was) that He is **slow to anger**. It is comforting to see how patient God was with Moses during his "wibble wobble" moments. Yet, let's not forget that He also punishes the guilty! Moses did finally go! And, the rest, as they say, is history!

What does Exodus 4:14 say about Aaron?

Let's bask in the knowledge that Aaron was already on his way! What does this tell you about God?

Let's close our time together by asking God to open the eyes of our hearts to see His plan and to tune our ears to His voice to hear His call! Commit to Him this day, if you're willing, "Here am I, send ME!"

---

[1] Morris
[2] Baker
[3] Butler
[4] Dockrey
[5] Goodrick
[6] Ibid
[7] The NIV Study Bible

Chapter 3:

Food For Thought

Day 1: Breakfast of Champions

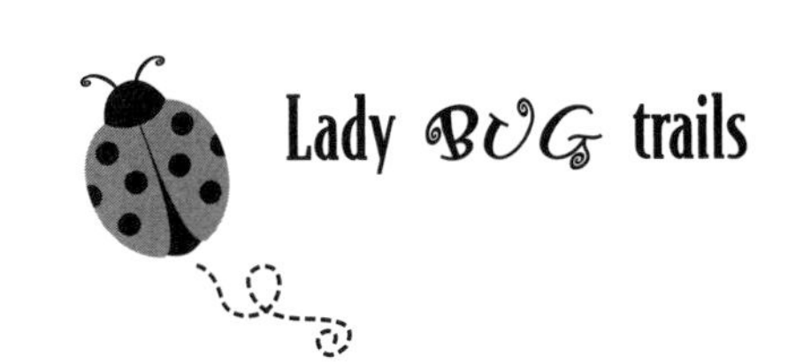

Lady BUG trails

Cereal to munch on: Wheaties

Snack to nibble on: 1 Timothy 4:8 Physical training is of some value, but godliness has value for all things, holding promise for both the present life and the life to come.

Very early in the morning, while it was still dark, I arose to write this lesson! ☺ As I perused the pantry for a fast, albeit nutritious breakfast, an orange cereal box - glowing in the dark - seemed to be whispering, "Pick me!" I picked up the box and wondered aloud, "WHEATIES the Breakfast of Champions. What's that about?"

According to the label this cereal is made with 100% whole grain! It is a good source of fiber and is low in fat. It provides the "champion's" body with complex carbs, which help fuel and re-energize tired muscles! This cereal is also rich in B-Vitamins, which help unlock the energy in food. Wheaties can help you reach your fitness goals! Tom Pappas, a former NCAA decathlon champion says, "There are no shortcuts to athletic success – it requires hard work and proper nutrition. Wheaties helps me get what I need to get the most out of my workouts." [1]

Here's some training advice from Tim Duncan, the basketball champion whose photo appears on the Wheaties box.

*"Love the journey and enjoy the process of the daily struggle. Stay focused and consistent **every day**, and most importantly, have fun!"*

Superb! Tim and I are on the same page! Here is Tim's training philosophy:

"Set both long and short-term goals. Know where you've been and where you want to go so that you can create a roadmap for success!" [2]

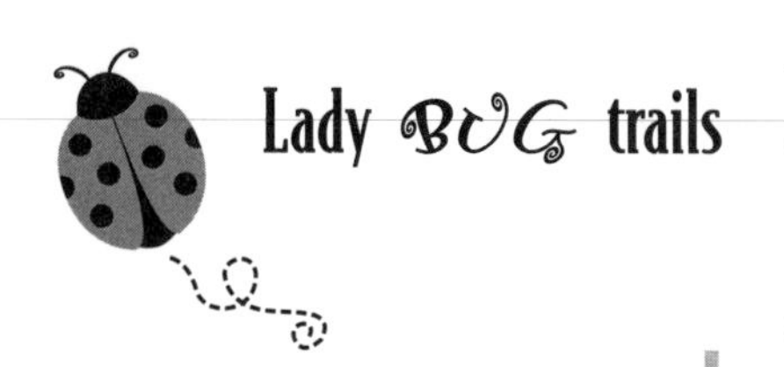

This is so important on our spiritual journey. My college professor often said, "Wherever you go, that's where you are." Yes, that is true. But, it's very important to know where we are going so we'll know where we are when we get there!

Read the following passage, examining it carefully with your magnifying glass. This is our TRAINING ADVICE for the day.

1 Timothy 4:7-8 (NIV)

In order to understand the context of this passage, we'll need to peek at a few other verses. Read 1 Timothy 1:1-7 (NIV).

Who is writing this letter? (v. 1) ______________________________

Who is the letter written to? (v. 2) ___________________________

Notice how Paul refers to Timothy as his "true son in the faith." WOW! What a validating greeting! Paul then encourages Timothy to stay in Ephesus so he can command certain men not to teach false doctrines nor "devote themselves to myths and endless genealogies."

According to verse 4, what do these promote? __________________

Now read 2 Timothy 4:3-4 (NIV). When people turn aside to myths, what are they turning away from? ______________________

Write 2 Timothy 2:15-16 in the space provided.

____

____

____

____

____

Zero in on verse 16. Those who indulge in godless chatter will become more and more ungodly! Grab your favorite highlighter or red pen and mark that truth!

Now, let's get back to our Training Advice. (1 Timothy 4:7-8) Paul is telling Timothy to steer clear of the myths. Instead, he wants Timothy to train himself to be godly! Verse 8 speaks to my heart deeply. Fill in the blanks.

Physical training is of __ __ __ __ value,

but __ __ __ __ __ __ __ __ __ has value for __ __ __ things,

holding promise for both the __ __ __ __ __ __ __ life

and the life to __ __ __ __!

This truth gives me chills on top of my goose bumps! Stop and think about this concept. America today is so "health" conscious! We go to the gym. We walk and jog. We do weight training. We drink lots of water. We limit our children's screen time and scoot them out of the house so they will exercise something other than their "mouse muscles" (playing computer games). But what about training ourselves to be godly? Is this something we do every day? What is godliness anyway? Remember the training philosophy of our Wheaties Champion, "Know where you've been and where you want to go so that you can create a roadmap for success!"

The original Greek word for godliness is *eusebeia*, which means "devout, godly; devotion, piety toward God." According to *The Complete Word Study Dictionary*, this word literally means "well-directed reverence; a life that is acceptable to Christ, indicating the proper attitude of the believer toward Christ who has saved him. It is both an attitude and a manner of life." [3]

Let's dig in the Word and find out more about godliness. Read these passages and write down a truth for each one.

1 Timothy 2:1-4

____

____

1 Timothy 6:3-11

____

____

2 Timothy 3:1-5

____

____

2 Peter 1:3-9

____

____

Lady BUG trails

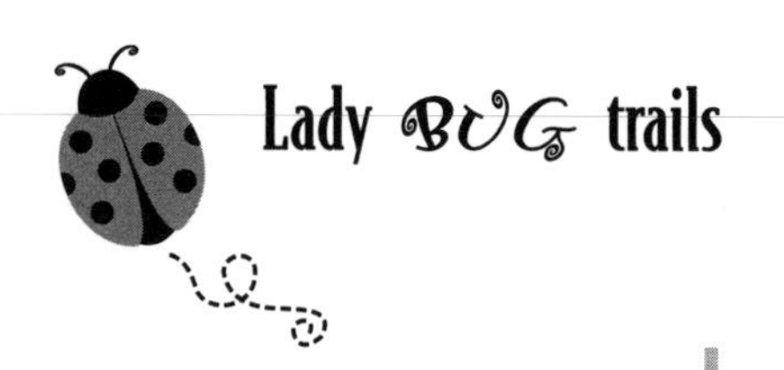

I hope you found some nutritious truth to chew on today. Here's one of my favorites. **Godliness with contentment is great gain!** (1 Timothy 6:6) Oh, how healthy we would be if we could ever learn the secret of being content as the apostle Paul did! Here are his words to the Philippians.

> **Philippians 4:12-13 (NIV)** I know what it is to be in need, and I know what it is to have plenty. I have learned the secret of being content in any and every situation, whether well fed or hungry, whether living in plenty or in want. I can do everything through him who gives me strength.

Contentment and Confidence with Christ! That, Lady BUG Sisters, is a fitness goal! Do these verses prick your heart? If so, explain.

____

____

Let's commit ourselves to consistent and DAILY training! We are not merely champions, we are more than CONQUERORS!

Write Romans 8:37.

____

____

____

What is the Breakfast of Conquerors? Wheaties of God! His Word provides us with 100% whole goodness. It fuels and re-energizes us! Look at this passage from the Amplified version of the Bible.

> **Hebrews 4:12 (AMP)** For the Word that God speaks is alive and full of power [making it active, operative, **energizing**, and effective]; it is sharper than any two-edged sword, penetrating to the dividing line of the breath of life (soul) and [the immortal] spirit, and of joints and marrow [of the deepest parts of our nature], exposing and sifting and analyzing and judging the very thoughts and purposes of the heart.

That is quite a mouthful! Read the passage again, then re-write the passage using language that you will remember!

The Word that God speaks is

The Word is rich in B vitamins! Check out the "B"eatitudes (Matthew 5:3-12). ☺ The Word of God can help you reach your fitness goals, especially if your goals include fighting the good fight, finishing the race, and keeping the faith! (See 2 Timothy 4:7.) Let's remember the training advice of our Wheaties Champion and apply it to our lives.

*"Love the journey and enjoy the process of the daily struggle. Stay focused and consistent **every day**, and most importantly, have fun!"*

Feeding on the Word of God can be a delicious and delightful experience! It doesn't have to be mundane. Write this psalm on a note card and hang it with your breakfast bowls.

Psalm 90:14 (NIV) Satisfy us in the morning with your unfailing love, that we may sing for joy and be glad all our days!

Let's consider this week how we can train ourselves to be godly. Let's remember that physical training is of "some value" but godliness has value for ALL things, in the present life and in the life to come! Invite your Almighty Personal Trainer to join you for breakfast. Let Him help you set some "fitness" goals. Praise Him for reminding us that Truth is Good FOOD!

Day 2: Living The Lyrics: Breathe

Before we begin, I'd like to make a special request. Please PRAY for God to administer CPR to your heart during this song. Ask Him to clear your air passages. Ask Him to free you from all distractions. Remember God's Word is alive and full of power! He will energize us if we let Him!

Sing the song. Belt it out! If you don't know the tune, God doesn't care. Just sing or say the lyrics or whisper them at the top of your lungs. **GO!** (And, please, let's not have a Moses Moment!) ☺

Breathe

(Words & music by Marie Barnett)

This is the air I breathe
This is the air I breathe
Your holy presence living in me

This is my daily bread
This is my daily bread
Your very Word spoken to me

And I, I'm desperate for You
And I, I'm lost without You, without You

(Repeat from beginning)

And I, I'm desperate for You
And I, I'm lost without You, without You

This is the air I breathe
This is the air I breathe

Record how you feel now.

I just love that song. It is so simple and yet, deeply profound. What is your favorite verse in the song? Why?

I happen to be sitting in my pajamas, feet propped up, with a box of Wheaties and coffee by my side. The flickering flame from the Lady BUG candle completes the ambience. Where are you? What are your surroundings?

Write 1 John 4:4 and celebrate this Fresh Breath of Truth!

Take a moment to digest the following line from the song.

"Your holy presence living in me."

Close your eyes. Breathe deeply and slowly. Check your pulse. Then, check it again. Are you being still? Are you choosing peace within? Do you feel His presence today? If so, tell Him how grateful you are. If not, ask Him why not? Go ahead...He'll draw near to you if you draw near to Him!

Let's take a closer look at the verse that so honestly admits, **"I'm desperate for You!"** Do you ever feel like you're gasping for air? You're afraid or unable to take a deep breath. David certainly felt "desperate" when he was in the cave crying out to God.

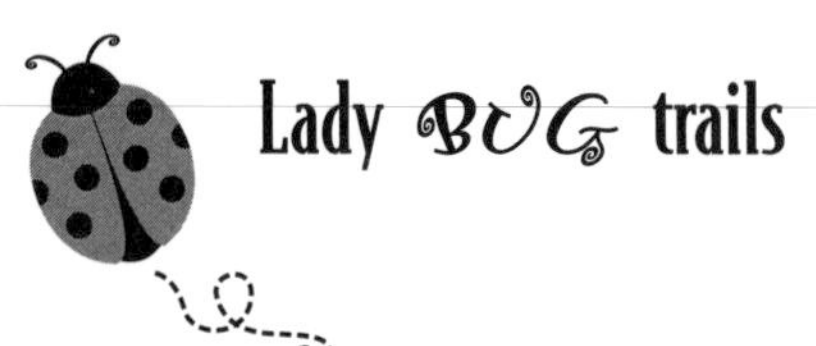

Read Psalm 142. I'm especially drawn to verse 6.

> "Listen to my cry, for I am in **desperate need**; rescue me from those who pursue me, for they are too strong for me."

Have you ever felt this way? If so, explain whatever you want to about it.

___

___

___

___

Asaph, one of David's choir leaders, makes a similar plea in Psalm 79:8. Fill in the blanks from the NIV. He asks,

> "May your mercy come quickly to meet us, for we are in
>
> ____________ ____________!"

Mull over this wonderful passage from The Message.

> ***When I was desperate, I called out, and GOD got me out of a tight spot! (Psalm 34:6 MSG)***

If you can think of a time when God did this for you, record it here. Remember to give Him all the glory!

___

___

___

___

John Scott (beloved pulpit minister for my home congregation) told a story one Sunday that prompted an enormous "Aha" moment for me. He quoted from a sermon he had heard by Dr. David O. Dykes entitled, "Thumbnails of Truth." Dr. Dykes attended his daughter's medical school graduation. The commencement speaker was Dr. Michael Palmer of Boston, a medical doctor and author. (You may be familiar with his best-selling medical thrillers!) Dr. Palmer spoke of his previous addiction to alcohol and prescription narcotics. He testified that he had "suffered in denial" for a long time! He then announced, **"One day I was given the wonderful GIFT of total desperation!"** He had finally hit rock bottom and when he did, he chose to get help! Dr. Palmer's suffering became his salvation! [4]

Whoa...have you ever put "total desperation" in the GIFT category? Reflect on Dr. Palmer's insightful words. How could total desperation be a gift? Can suffering be our salvation, too? No right or wrong answers...just jot down your first thoughts.

____

____

____

____

Read Romans 5:1-5. What does suffering produce? What does perseverance produce? What does character produce? Use your artistic abilities and draw a flow chart with arrows depicting the "production line." (Have fun with it. You don't have to turn it in for a grade!)

Now, take a look at that! HOPE is at the end of the line! Don't we all want and need hope? It's important to notice that the text says for us to rejoice IN our sufferings not "because of" our sufferings. What's the difference?

____

____

Where do we go when we're in desperate need; when we're gasping for air? We go to the Only One who can provide true oxygen for our souls. He will give us a "breathing treatment" like no other.

Day 3: Breath of Fresh Air

Snack to nibble on: 2 Timothy 3:16 (NIV) All Scripture is God-breathed!

CPR. What is the first thing that pops into your mind when you see those three letters together?

____

The *Encyclopaedia Britannica* defines CPR as "cardiopulmonary resuscitation." CPR is "an emergency procedure designed to restore normal breathing and circulation after such traumas as cardiac arrest and drowning. CPR involves clearing the air passages to the lungs and carrying out external heart massage by the exertion of pressure on the chest." [5]

Read the definition again. Specifically, what is CPR designed to do? What does CPR involve?

____

____

The **first step** in CPR is to open the airway by placing the individual on his back on a rigid surface, clearing foreign matter from the mouth or airway, and tilting the head back so that the chin is elevated.

The **second step** involves mouth-to-mouth resuscitation —clamping the victim's nostrils, making an airtight seal over his mouth and breathing into it about 12 times per minute, allowing for natural exhalation.

The **third step** is to check one of the carotid arteries (large blood vessels located on either side of the voice box) for a pulse. Absence of a pulse requires artificial circulation of the blood by means of external chest compressions (at the rate of about 80 per minute for adults). The recommended ratio of chest compressions to breaths administered is 15:2. CPR should continue uninterrupted until normal breathing and circulation are restored or until advanced professional medical assistance can be obtained. [6]

In simple phrases you can easily remember, list the three steps of CPR below:

1.

2.

3.

If you attend my home congregation, **CPR** might remind you of our wonderful summer outreach program called **C**are, **P**lay, & **R**ead where volunteers care for kids, play with kids, and read with kids. God's Word is taught to these children every day, and in many cases, His Word restores free breathing and massages their hearts! Lives are being changed. Souls are being saved. This ministry, in effect, performs emergency procedures on families every day!

Get comfy and breathe easy. Relax and give yourself the gift of calm. Today we're going to inhale God's Word. Let's begin with some "breath" and "breathe" passages.

> Genesis 2:7 (AMP) Then the Lord God formed man from the dust of the ground and breathed into his nostrils the breath or spirit of life, and man became a living being.

Circle the part of the scripture that is most intriguing to you. Contemplate why you chose that word or phrase. Explain.

____

____

Read Job 32:8. Where do we get our understanding?

____

____

Read Job 33:4. What does the breath of the Almighty give us? What does this mean to you?

____

____

Let's pay close attention to the following verses from the Amplified Bible.

> **2 Timothy 3:16-17 (AMP)** Every Scripture is God-breathed (given by His inspiration) and profitable for instruction, for reproof and conviction of sin, for correction of error and discipline in obedience, [and] for training in righteousness (in holy living, in conformity to God's will in thought, purpose, and action), So that the man of God may be complete and proficient, well fitted and thoroughly equipped for every good work.

The original Greek word translated "God-breathed" is *theopneustos*, which combines Theos (God) and Pneo (to breathe or blow). Theopneustos means

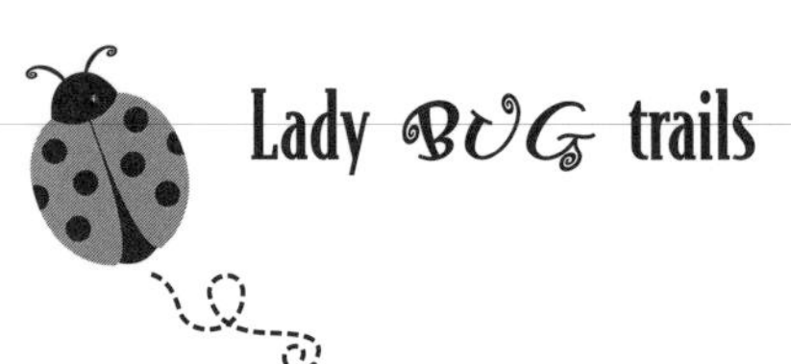

"prompted by God, divinely inspired."[7] The only place this word is found in the New Testament is in 2 Timothy 3:16.

Meditate on the truth that every Scripture is prompted by God and divinely inspired. Does this impact the way you view the Bible? Explain.

____

____

Verse 17 tells us the purpose of God-breathed Scripture.
He wants us to be complete.
He wants us to be proficient.
He wants us to be well-fitted.
He wants us to be thoroughly equipped.

The New Living Translation sums it up nicely by saying God-breathed Scripture is "God's way of preparing us in every way!" (2 Timothy 3:17, NLT)

Spend the rest of your study time in prayerful consideration. Personalize what we've learned today. Allow God's Word to perform cardiopulmonary resuscitation on YOU! Remember those three steps?

1. Allow God to open your airway. He may have to clear some "foreign matter" to do so! List the "foreign matter" that might be blocking your airway.

____

____

2. Engage in Mouth-to-Mouth Resuscitation. Explore what this means spiritually. Who? What? Where? When? Why? How?

____

____

____

3. Check your pulse – spiritually! Does your heart need a few compressions? No Rules...Just Write!

____

____

____

Close by thanking God for His precious, life-altering Word that is a much-needed BREATH OF FRESH AIR!

Day 4: Living the Lyrics: Breathe On Me

Huff puff, huff puff! We live in a plate-spinning, ball-juggling, treadmill-running, roller-coaster-riding world. Sometimes I come to a screeching halt and say, "Wait! Give me a minute to catch my breath!"

Ponder for a moment. What does the phrase "catch my breath" really mean?

____

____

____

Write Jeremiah 31:25.

____

____

____

God's refreshment is like no other! If you've ever been on an airplane you know that the flight attendant always reminds us to place the oxygen mask on our own face before we put one on our child. The same is true when we're in spiritual crisis.

Someone wise once said,

It is impossible to give away what we do not possess!

Do you agree? Share your thoughts on this subject.

____

____

____

____

____

____

If a friend or family member needs a breath of fresh air from me, I must first fill myself up. How do I do that?

____

____

____

Think about this concept as you sing this beautiful song.

Breathe On Me

(Words & music by Matt Huesmann and Grant Cunningham)

Breathe on me breath of God
Bring my life close to Your Spirit
Beat in me heart of God
My soul's in prayer to be near it
Focus my eyes
To only see what's You
And breathe on me
Breathe on me breath of God

Breathe on me breath of God
I am a vessel to be filled
Comfort me peace of God
Lord, I am restless for Your will
Silence my fears
So that I may hear from You
And breathe on me
Breathe on me breath of God

Surround me in Your glory
Make Your presence known
Set the path of grace before me
Let Your breath become my own

Breathe on me breath of God
Cover my sin with Your mercy
Speak to me Word of God
Give me a light for my journey
Show me Your way
And draw me close to You
And breathe on me
Breathe on me
Breathe on me breath of God

Now, take a highlighter or red pen and circle the phrase or verse that touches you most. What is your heart's response? Why did you pick that particular phrase? No Rules...Just Write!

Read John 20:19-22. Imagine what it must have been like to be in that room...to see what the disciples saw...to hear what they heard...to feel what they felt! Imagine Jesus HIMSELF fresh out of the tomb breathing on YOU! How would you feel? What would your reaction be?

What was the first thing Jesus said to them? (Notice He said this twice!)

Write John 20:21-22.

How do we receive the Holy Spirit today? (See Acts 2:38)

Read Romans 8:9-11. Slowly read and absorb verse 11 from The Message.

It stands to reason, doesn't it, that if the alive-and-present God who raised Jesus from the dead moves into your life, he'll do the same thing in you that he did in Jesus, bringing you alive to himself? **When God lives and breathes in you (and he does, as surely as he did in Jesus), you are delivered from that dead life.** With his Spirit living in you, your body will be as alive as Christ's!

Inhale the TRUTH in these verses. What does this mean for your life?

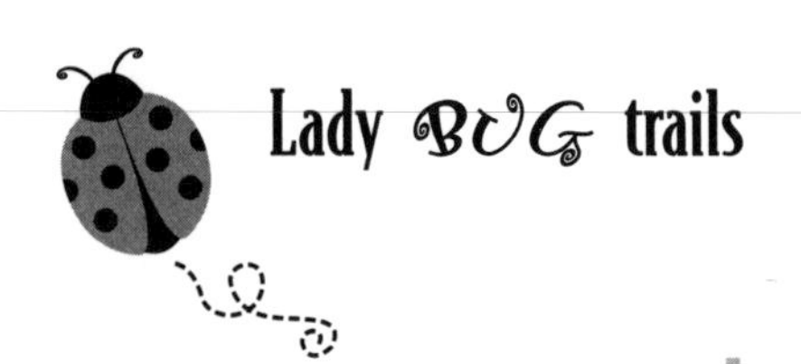

Dig in the Word for some other scriptures that confirm the truth found in this beautiful song. (For example, you might find a scripture for "give me a light for my journey" or scriptures teaching about "peace" or "mercy.") Have FUN with it! Delight in it! Remember, if you delight yourself in the Lord He will give you the desires of your heart! (Psalm 37:4) Take a deep breath and say Ahhhhhhhhhhhhh!

____

____

____

____

____

____

---

[1] Wheaties box
[2] Ibid
[3] Zodhiates
[4] Dykes, Dr. David O.
[5] Cardiopulmonary resuscitation
[6] Ibid
[7] Zodhiates

Chapter 4:

Truth is Good Food

Day 1: Our Daily Bread

Lady BUG trails

Snack to nibble on: Job 23:12 (NIV) I have treasured the words of his mouth more than my daily bread.

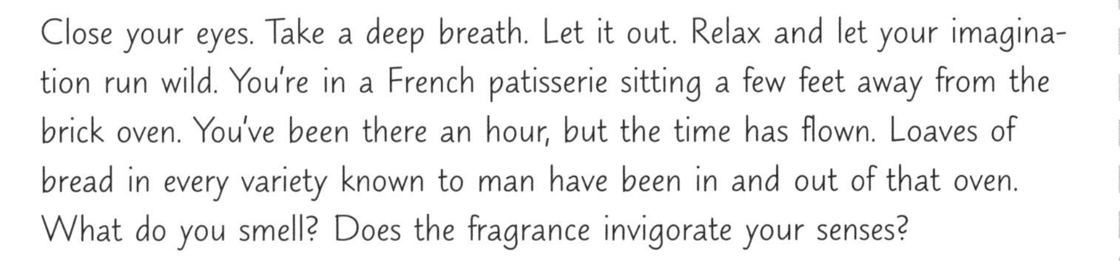

Close your eyes. Take a deep breath. Let it out. Relax and let your imagination run wild. You're in a French patisserie sitting a few feet away from the brick oven. You've been there an hour, but the time has flown. Loaves of bread in every variety known to man have been in and out of that oven. What do you smell? Does the fragrance invigorate your senses?

____

____

I'll tell you a secret. My nose hairs rise up and do a celebration squiggle dance when I'm in the presence of freshly baked bread. There's just something about it. Mmmm...Mmmm...good!

Today we've got lots of reading to do. Why? Because the Word of God is FULL of scriptures about bread. Bread from heaven. Bread of God. Bread of Life. Bread of Truth. Daily bread. And, the list goes on and on.

Remember the great lyrics to the song, Breathe? Hopefully by now you've got it memorized. If not, take out the lyrics and sing it once more.

This is my daily bread
This is my daily bread
Your very Word spoken to me!

Remember our friend, Moses, who we left back at the bush? If we fast forward past his trip to Egypt, past the plagues, past the part where Pharaoh finally let the people GO, and past the part where they walked through the Red Sea (on dry ground!) we will find Moses and the Israelites in the desert. It's been exactly one month since they left Egypt.

Lady BUG trails

Read Exodus 16:1-35.

Manna. Vines dictionary describes it as "the supernaturally provided food for Israel during their wilderness journey." [1] It's described in Psalm 78:24, 25 as the "grain of heaven." Apparently, it was small and round. We'll never know exactly what it looked like or tasted like because it was a supernatural GIFT for them! We are given a few clues, though. According to Exodus 16:31, what did manna look like? What did it taste like?

____

____

In Numbers 11:4-9 we hear the Israelites grumbling about the manna. This gives us a few more details about their "miracle food."

What did it look like? (v. 7) How did they grind and cook it?

____

____

What did it taste like? When did the manna come?

____

____

Read Deuteronomy 8:2-3.

What lesson did God teach with the manna?

____

____

I love the fact that God caused them to HUNGER and then He fed them! This reminds me of one of our "B" vitamins in the Word. Write Matthew 5:6 on the lines below.

____

____

____

Rest assured, when we hunger and thirst after righteousness He will fill us! I find comfort in that fact. Do you? If so, share your feelings in the Lady BUG trail margin.

Read Matthew 4:1-4.

Who led Jesus into the desert to be tempted?____________________

How long did Jesus fast?____________________________________

Notice the last 3 words of verse 2. **He was hungry!** What is the difference between physical hunger and spiritual hunger?

____

____

Practically speaking, how do we live on God's Word?

____

____

Often, we attempt to satisfy our spiritual hunger with something other than God's Word. Name a few of those substitutes.

____

____

Jesus explains in the book of John that HE is, indeed, the Bread of Life. He does such a fabulous job explaining Himself (He is, after all, the greatest Teacher that ever lived) that I would like you to get comfy, grab a highlighter, and just sit at His feet and FEED. As you graze, highlight the Words you want to ingest and digest!

John 6:25-58 (NIV) Jesus the Bread of Life

25 When they found him on the other side of the lake, they asked him, "Rabbi, when did you get here?" 26 Jesus answered, "I tell you the truth, you are looking for me, not because you saw miraculous signs but because you ate the loaves and had your fill. 27 Do not work for food that spoils, but **for food that endures to eternal life**, which the Son of Man will give you. On him God the Father has placed his seal of approval." 28Then they asked him, "What must we do to do the works God requires?" 29 Jesus answered, "The work of God is this: to believe in the one he has sent." 30 So they asked him, "What miraculous sign then will you give that we may see it and believe you? What will you do? 31 Our forefathers ate the manna in the desert; as it is written: **'He gave them bread from heaven to eat.'**" 32 Jesus said to them, "I tell you the truth, it is not Moses who has given you the bread from heaven, **but it is my Father who gives you the true bread from heaven.** 33 **For the bread of God is he who comes down from heaven and gives life to the world.**" 34 "Sir," they

said, "**from now on give us this bread.**" 35 Then Jesus declared, "**I am the bread of life**. He who comes to me will never go hungry, and he who believes in me will never be thirsty. 36 But as I told you, you have seen me and still you do not believe. 37 All that the Father gives me will come to me, and whoever comes to me I will never drive away. 38 For I have come down from heaven not to do my will but to do the will of him who sent me. 39 And this is the will of him who sent me, that I shall lose none of all that he has given me, but raise them up at the last day. 40 For my Father's will is that everyone who looks to the Son and believes in him shall have eternal life, and I will raise him up at the last day." 41 At this the Jews began to grumble about him because he said, "**I am the bread that came down from heaven.**" 42 They said, "Is this not Jesus, the son of Joseph, whose father and mother we know? How can he now say, 'I came down from heaven'?" 43 "Stop grumbling among yourselves," Jesus answered. 44 "No one can come to me unless the Father who sent me draws him, and I will raise him up at the last day. 45 It is written in the Prophets: 'They will all be taught by God.' Everyone who listens to the Father and learns from him comes to me. 46 No one has seen the Father except the one who is from God; only he has seen the Father. 47 I tell you the truth, he who believes has everlasting life. 48 **I am the bread of life.** 49 **Your forefathers ate the manna in the desert, yet they died.** 50 **But here is the bread that comes down from heaven, which a man may eat and not die.** 51 I am the **living bread** that came down from heaven. If anyone eats of this bread, he will live forever. This bread is my flesh, which I will give for the life of the world." 52 Then the Jews began to argue sharply among themselves, "How can this man give us his flesh to eat?" 53 Jesus said to them, "I tell you the truth, unless you eat the flesh of the Son of Man and drink his blood, you have no life in you. 54 **Whoever eats my flesh and drinks my blood has eternal life, and I will raise him up at the last day.** 55 **For my flesh is real food and my blood is real drink.** 56 **Whoever eats my flesh and drinks my blood remains in me, and I in him.** 57 Just as the living Father sent me and I live because of the Father, so the one who feeds on me will live because of me. 58 This is the bread that came down from heaven. Your forefathers ate manna and died, **but he who feeds on this bread will live forever."**

Notice the question asked in verse 28. Sometimes I feel like asking the same question today! Write Christ's answer (verse 29) below.

____

____

What more can be said? Pass the Bread! I'm famished! How about you? Did the Words of Christ speak directly to your heart? If so, tell Him. He would love to hear from you! No matter how you slice it, Truth Is Good Food!

Give us today our daily bread! Matthew 6:11

Day 2: Living the Lyrics: Take Time to Be Holy

There's an old, old song that I've been singing since I was knee-high to a grasshopper. Perhaps you know it, too.

Sing the song below. Meditate on each line. Remember our goal in learning new songs and revisiting old songs is to LIVE THE LYRICS!

Take Time To Be Holy

(Words: W.D. Longstaff; Music: Geo. C. Stebbins)

Take time to be holy
Speak oft with thy Lord
Abide in Him always
And feed on His Word
Make friends of God's children
Help those who are weak
Forgetting in nothing
His blessings to seek

Take time to be holy
The world rushes on
Spend much time in secret
With Jesus alone
Abiding in Jesus
Like Him thou shalt be
Thy friends in thy conduct
His likeness shall see

Take time to be holy
Be calm in thy soul
Each thought and each motive
Beneath His control
Thus led by His Spirit
To fountains of love
Thou soon shall be fitted
For service above

W.D. Longstaff wrote this song in the late 1800s so it is full of archaic phrases. Highlight or circle some of the phrases we rarely use in modern times. Then list them below re-writing the archaic phrases using modern language. (The first one has been done for you in case you'd like an example.)

Archaic phrase	Modern Language
Speak oft with thy Lord.	Communicate with God often.

Recently, this song has become very special to me. Several days this week I've woken up with it on my mind!

Read **Isaiah 50:4 (NIV)** and fill in these blanks.

The Sovereign LORD has given me an ____________________

tongue, to know the __________ that sustains the weary. He

wakens me _________________ by _________________, wakens

my ear to __________ like one being taught!

Lady BUG Sisters, I believe with all my heart that God wants us to tune our ears, especially in the morning! Have you ever woken up with a song on your mind; a scripture on your tongue; or a truth on your heart? If so, write down everything you can remember about it.

____

____

____

____

____

____

____

____

____

Become aware of your morning messages. LISTEN to them! Perhaps God is giving you some instructions. He's giving you a Word that will sustain you or someone in your life! I believe God has been waking me up with this song so that I would dig a little deeper and find some treasures. Let's dig in together.

Take time to be HOLY!

Whoa...this first line stops me in my tracks. Holy is such an awe-inspiring word. It's easy to think of God as being holy. It's quite another to think of ME that way! Read the following passages and note what you learn.

1 Corinthians 1:2

____

____

____

Ephesians 1:4

____

____

____

1 Thessalonians 4:4-7

____

____

____

2 Timothy 1:9

____

____

____

Hebrews 12:14

____

____

____

1 Peter 1:15-16

____

____

____

2 Peter 3:11

The Greek word for "holy" in this context is ***hagios***, which means "any matter of religious awe, expiation, sacrifice; holy, set apart, sanctified, consecrated, saint. Its fundamental idea is separation, consecration, and devotion to the service of Deity, sharing in God's purity and abstaining from earth's defilement. Metaphorically it means morally pure, upright, blameless in heart and life, and virtuous!" [2]

Write the definition of *hagios* in YOUR OWN WORDS.

According to the Scriptures, we are ***called*** to be holy! He chose us before the creation of the world to be holy. It is God's will for us to live a holy life. God wants us to make "every effort" to live in peace with all men and to be holy! Pay close attention to the last half of Hebrews 12:14—"without holiness no one will see the Lord!" Yikes! Does this prick your heart?

God wants us to be holy in all we do. He wants us to be holy because He is holy! He tells us to live holy and godly lives as we look forward to the day of God and speed its coming!

So...His morning message is coming in loud and clear!!! But how do we go about doing this?

Get down on your knees and bow before the Father today asking Him to show you ONE WAY you can be more holy this week.

Lady BUG trails

Lady BUG trails

Day 3: It's About Time!

Snack to nibble on: Ecclesiastes 3:1 There is a time for everything, and a season for every activity under heaven.

Usually we spend one day studying the lyrics to a song. The song "Take Time To Be Holy," however, will take us the rest of the week!

Take TIME to be holy!

We all have 24 hours in the day. Right? So, it's not a matter of making the time (God has already done that for us.) It's a matter of ***taking the time***!

Read Ecclesiastes 3:1-8.

How does this passage speak to your heart?

____

____

____

Pick a day last week...say, Tuesday or Thursday, whichever you prefer. How did you spend your time? Be specific! Write down times and actual happenings. Where did you go? What did you do? Did you eat three meals sitting down? Eat on the run? Who did you interact with? What time did you get up? What time did you go to bed? (There will be no judging or comparing so just write down the facts!) Use your Lady BUG trails margin.

Now, glance back over the list. Did you sit on the couch all day watching TV and eating bonbons? Did you stare into space because you were bored out of your mind with nothing to do? Did you take care of your own needs and nobody else's?

____

____

I wish I could read each answer. But, chances are HIGH that many of you (if not most) looked back over your day and saw a BUSY BEE! Now, hear this!! **To God be the glory for that!** If you had nothing to write in the blanks then you'd likely be one depressed blob! Allow me to get on my soapbox for a moment. In my opinion, the word "busy" is one of the most abused buzz words in the English language! I know a neat freak husband who quotes Titus 2:5 (women should be "busy" at home) in order to guilt his wife into keeping an immaculate home. He feels she is neglecting her Christian duty if she leaves dishes in the sink for a few hours after dinner or gets a day behind on the laundry. In his world, BUSY = GOOD CHRISTIAN.

On the other hand, over and over again I have heard B-U-S-Y used as an acronym for BUSY. [3]

Being
Under
Satan's
Yoke

The person who coined this acronym obviously believes that
BUSY = BAD CHRISTIAN.

So...who's right? Does being busy make me a good Christian or a bad Christian? (Take a Lady BUG trail if you need more room to answer!)

____

____

Call me crazy and put me in the loony bin but here's my answer to the question, "Who's right?" I shout a resounding BOTH and NEITHER! In my opinion being busy is not the issue.

Read the following verse from the Amplified Bible.

> **2 Corinthians 5:10 (Amplified Bible)** For we must all appear and be revealed as we are before the judgment seat of Christ, so that each one may receive [his pay] according to what he has done in the body, whether good or evil [considering what his purpose and motive have been, and what he has achieved, been busy with, and given himself and his attention to accomplishing].

Based on this scripture I see a great way to take a quick peek at the way we've been spending our time.

What was my purpose?
What was my motive?
What was I hoping to achieve?
What have I been busy with?
What have I been giving my whole self to?
What have I been devoting my attention to?

Lady BUG trails

God certainly does not want us to "eat the bread of idleness." (See Proverbs 31:27) Yet, He also knows we will choke to death if we choose the bread of busyness instead of the Bread of Life!

Read Luke 10:38-42. Let's examine verse 40 in the Amplified Bible.

But Martha [overly occupied and too busy] was distracted with much serving; and she came up to Him and said, Lord, is it nothing to You that my sister has left me to serve alone? Tell her then to help me [to lend a hand and do her part along with me]!

The text says Martha was "overly occupied and too busy." What was she distracted with? (Write it in big, bold letters!)

MUCH _ _ _ _ _ _ _!

Ouch! My tootsies are throbbing. Those words stomp all over my toes and my heart! How many times in my life have I been distracted with much serving?! How about you? Can you relate?

____

____

____

Write the words of Christ below. Imagine that He is speaking these words to your heart at this moment! Write Luke 10:41-42. Replace "Martha, Martha" with your own name!

____

____

____

____

____

Remember our nugget of truth "without holiness no one will see the Lord!" What on earth could be more important than taking the time to be holy?! **Mary knew that a woman's place in the home is at the feet of Jesus!**

Take a moment and consider how you will commit to "taking the time." Do you spend time with God daily? If so, when and where? If not...be honest...why not? Please don't write what you're "supposed" to say! Write what your heart says. Take your time. This bit of the journey is well worth taking a pit stop. Ponder and pray. Use your Lady BUG trails margin.

Speak oft with thy Lord!

Remember our modern phrase for this archaic message? Communicate with God often! What is your own personal definition of prayer?

Read the following verses about prayer and jot down what you want to remember about each one!

Matthew 6:5-15

Mark 11:20-26

Luke 18:1-8 (Note the purpose for this parable in v. 1!)

Ephesians 6:18

1 Thessalonians 3:10 (Notice how and how often Paul prayed.)

1 Thessalonians 5:16-18

James 5:13-18

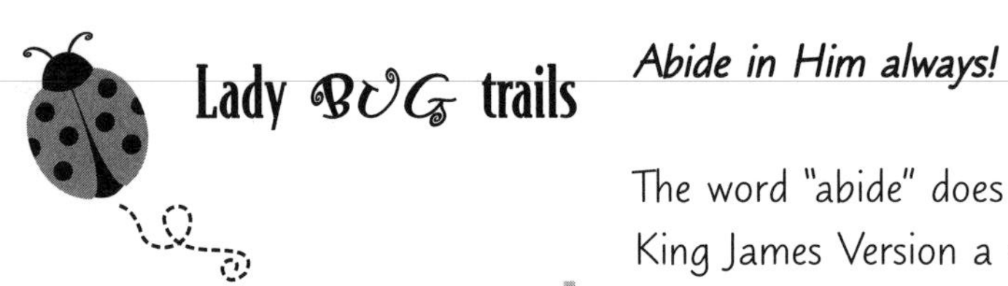

Abide in Him always!

The word "abide" does not appear in the NIV Bible, but it does appear in the King James Version a whopping 103 times! Since we may not have time to read all 103 (ha) we'll just look at a few. Summarize these verses in your own words.

John 15:1-17 (NIV uses "remain"; KJV uses "abide")

____

____

____

Look back over your notes from today. What is ONE THING you better understand about God?

____

____

____

Day 4: Feed On His Word!

Lady BUG trails

Snack to nibble on: John 4:34 (NIV) "My food," said Jesus, "is to do the will of Him who sent me and to finish His work."

Feed on His Word!

This is my favorite passage in the whole song. (Hence, the title of this lesson!) Sisters, lean in so you can hear my whole heart! God's Word is nourishment for our souls! Remember what Job said? "I have treasured the words of His mouth more than my daily bread!" (Job 23:12) Jesus said something similar and soooooo profound. Read John 4:27-34.

Write John 4:32 and 34.

____

____

____

Now, go back and look at it. (Yes, you can use your magnifying glass to eagerly examine this one!) Jesus says His **food** is:

To do God's will
To finish His work

That's what I call WHOLE FOOD! Remember what Jesus said when He was hungry in the desert? The tempter wanted Him to turn stones into bread and Jesus quoted what Moses had told the Israelites, "Man does not live on bread alone but on every word that comes from the mouth of the Lord." (Matthew 4:4)

If we truly want to do what Jesus did (not just wear the WWJD® bracelets, but actually live the life!) this is the perfect formula for us! We nourish ourselves by doing God's will and finishing His work! How do we find out what God's will is for our lives?

We eat His Words!!!

According to John 6:35-40, what is God's will?

____

____

____

Read 1 Thessalonians 4:3-8. What is God's will?

See 1 Thessalonians 5:16-18. What is God's will for you?

According to 1 Peter 2:15, what is God's will?

How can I be a "sister" to Christ? See Mark 3:31-35.

How will I be able to test and approve what God's will is? See Romans 12:1-2.

Read Philippians 2:12-18. Write the treasures of truth you find!

Rejoice while reading 1 John 2:17. Write the waaaay cool part!

May we live as Jesus lived and speak as Jesus spoke. Find a prominent place in your kitchen, car, or study area for the following verse. Read it every day. Recite it out loud! You'll be amazed at how one small verse can make an enormous change in your life! (It will be especially helpful for those Moses Moments!) Personalize it with your first and last name. **Hebrews 10:7, 9**

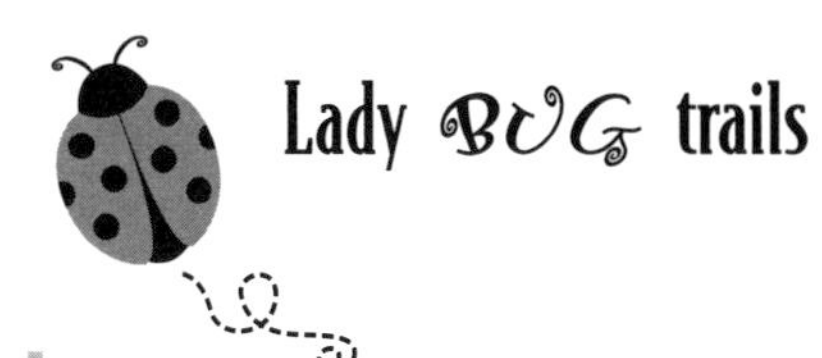

Here I am, I, ______________________________ have come to do your will, O God!

We can also find comfort that, like Jesus, we are able to finish God's work! Read Philippians 1:1-6. Fill in these blanks from verse 6. (NIV)

He who began a ____________ ____________ in you will carry it on to ______________________________ until the day of Christ Jesus.

Did you need to hear this truth today? Is there a particular "unfinished" work in your life that you are eager for God to complete? Explain!

____

____

____

____

____

Make friends of God's children!

How were the early Christians instructed to greet one another?

____

(See Romans 16:16; 1 Corinthians 16:20; 2 Corinthians 13:12; 1 Thessalonians 5:26)

According to the *Complete Word Study Dictionary*, the holy kiss means "the sacred Christian kiss, the pledge of Christian affection!" [4]

What are the benefits of making friends with God's children?

____

____

____

____

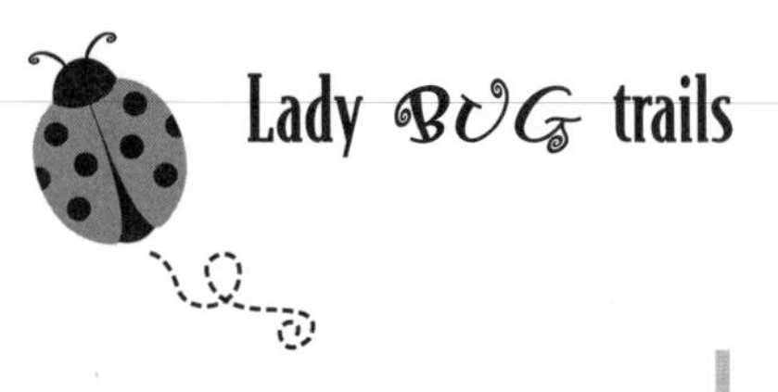

Help those who are weak!

Read 1 Thessalonians 5:12-15. Record your favorite parts!

What is the difference between "helping" the weak and "rescuing" the weak? No rules...Just Write!

Forgetting in nothing His blessings to seek!

Take time to be holy. It's worth every minute! Pour out your heart in prayer. Praise Him for your blessings. (Count them one by one!) ☺ Pig out on His smorgasbord of Truth this week. Your hunger will be satisfied like never before. Always remember that Truth Is Good Food!

Psalm 119:20 (MSG) My soul is starved and hungry, ravenous! It's insatiable for your nourishing commands

---

[1] Vine
[2] Zodhiates
[3] Acronym Finder
[4] Zodhiates

Chapter 5:

The Original Lady BUG

Day 1: Her Namesake

Question to ponder: Do you know how the ladybug got its name?

Snack to nibble on: Luke 1:26-27 (NIV) God sent the angel Gabriel to Nazareth...to a virgin...named Mary.

Mom says I came out of the womb asking questions. She says I startled the doctor the day I was born asking, "Hey, why did you spank me on the derriere?" Do you agree that her statement is preposterous? Why would she ever say a thing like that? Be honest. Do you think I ask too many questions? Or, here's a better question. Could there be such a thing as too many questions? ☺

Here's a question for you. Do you know how the ladybug got its name? Well, if you don't, you are in for a real treat! A few months ago I was doing a little Lady BUG research when I came across a piece of information I'd never seen before. Tradition says in Europe, during the Middle Ages, many crops were being destroyed by swarms of insects. The Catholic farmers, desperate to save their crops, prayed to the Virgin Mary for HELP! Not long after their cry for help, beautiful beneficial beetles appeared. They devoured the pests that had been destroying the farmers' crops and saved the day! The farmers nicknamed these insects "The Beetles of Our Lady." Later, the name was shortened to "Lady Beetles" and then eventually shortened to "ladybugs!" Some say the red wings represented the Virgin Mary's cloak. The black spots symbolized both her joys and her sorrows. [1]

This prompted me to retreat to my thoughtful <u>spot</u>. **The Virgin Mary.** I never had a clue that these cute little creatures were actually named after the mother of Christ! Have you ever heard this before? Then, the questions began to swirl! (Ok, Mom, maybe you're right about the questions!) I vividly remember to this day the inquisition that took place in my mind.

So...what do I really know about Mary? Why don't I know more about her? Who were Mary's parents? How old was she when she became pregnant? I

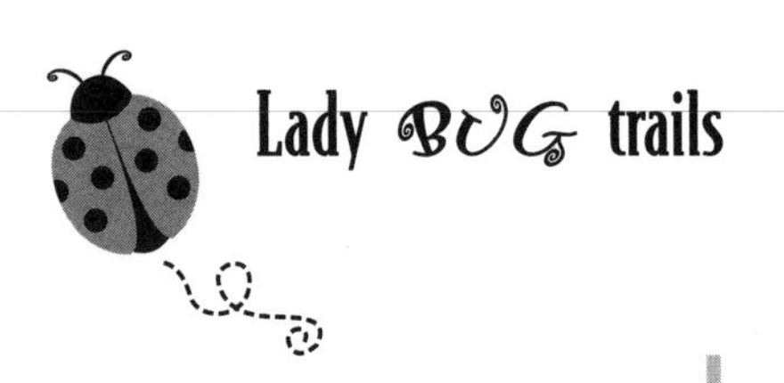

know Matthew and Luke give us some tidbits about her life. Does Mark mention her? John gives us the wedding at Cana and the scene at the foot of the cross. Paul never mentions her, or does he? How was Mary related to Elizabeth? Where was Mary born? How did she die?

Stop and consider what you know about Mary, the mother of Jesus. Quickly jot down everything you know about her from memory. If questions pop up, list those, too. Don't peek in your Bible, yet. We'll do plenty of that later. Use the Lady BUG trails margin to jot down your thoughts.

Is your list full of facts or questions? Over the years I've been exposed to many "Marys." There's the **"Museum Mary"** I've seen in paintings, sculptures, and statues. There's the **"Miniature Mary"** I've seen in hundreds of nativity scenes. **"Miracle Mary"** is prayed to in the last few seconds of a football game. (A "Hail Mary pass" is usually made in desperation at the end of a game. This phrase was made most popular by Dallas Cowboys quarterback Roger Staubach. After his famous game-winning touchdown pass to Drew Pearson in the 1975 NFC Championship game, Roger told the press, "I closed my eyes and said a "Hail Mary.") [2] Let's not forget **"Mystical Merchandise Mary"** emblazoned on a grilled cheese sandwich that sold on eBay for $28,000. [3] What about the phrase **"Mary, Mother of God"** that is flippantly shouted when somebody stumps his toe? Hollywood has really latched on to that phrase! They think it's too hilarious. I fail to find the humor!

Does this BUG you like it does me? What other "Marys" have you been exposed to?

____

____

Enough already! I simply want to learn more about Mary, the mother of Jesus, the REAL woman. I want to "treasure up" all the truth about Mary from the Word of God and ponder these truths in my heart! ☺ Do you? If so, grab your spade and let's head to the garden to do a little gardening with God. We're going to dig deep in the scriptures and see what we can unearth today. Let's begin by reading the first few tidbits that Dr. Luke gives us about Mary.

Read Luke 1:26-28 (NIV).

According to the NIV Study Bible, "in the sixth month" simply means "from the time of John the Baptist's conception" (see Luke 1:36). [4] In order to understand the context we'll need to peek into the lives of Zechariah and Elizabeth, Mary's relative. It is not known for sure whether Elizabeth was Mary's cousin, aunt, or other relation.

Read Luke 1:5-25. (NIV)

How long did Elizabeth remain in seclusion after she became pregnant? (v. 24)

____

In the sixth month God sent an angel. What was the angel's name? (v. 26) ____________________________ Notice this is the same angel that appeared to Zechariah! (Luke 1:19)

Lean back in your chair and relax. Let's do a little experiment. When you hear the word "angel" what comes to mind? Close your eyes and focus on the image you see. Describe the angel in detail. Take your time.

____

____

____

I would love to read every single description. Chances are they would vary from person to person. In the art world we find chubby bare-bottom baby angels and dazzling women angels with long flowing hair. This week I took a Lady BUG trail down Angel Lane and looked up every verse in the Bible that contained the word angel. That was quite an eye-opening experience! You might want to take a Lady BUG trail down Angel Lane yourself!

The *Complete Word Study Dictionary* describes Gabriel as "an angel especially entrusted with the message to Zechariah concerning the birth of John, and to Mary concerning the birth of Christ (Luke 1:19-26). At an earlier period, he was sent to Daniel to unfold a vision (Daniel 8:16; 9:21). One of the two angels referred to [by name] in the Bible, the other being Michael the archangel (Jude 1:9) who is the warrior angel." [5]

Let's pause to think about the enormity of this truth. There are thousands upon thousands of angels (Matthew 26:53; Hebrews 12:22; Revelation 5:11-12). We only know two by name. It fascinates me that Gabriel introduced himself by name to Zechariah (see Luke 1:19). As far as we know, he did NOT introduce himself by name to Mary but we are told that it's Gabriel. Just for fun, read Daniel 9:20-23.

How did Gabriel come to Daniel? ________________________________

Whoa. He came to Daniel in "swift flight." The Amplified Bible says, "Gabriel, being caused to fly swiftly, came near to me..." This tickles me. Why? There are <u>many</u> scriptures describing the winged cherubim or living creatures. There are

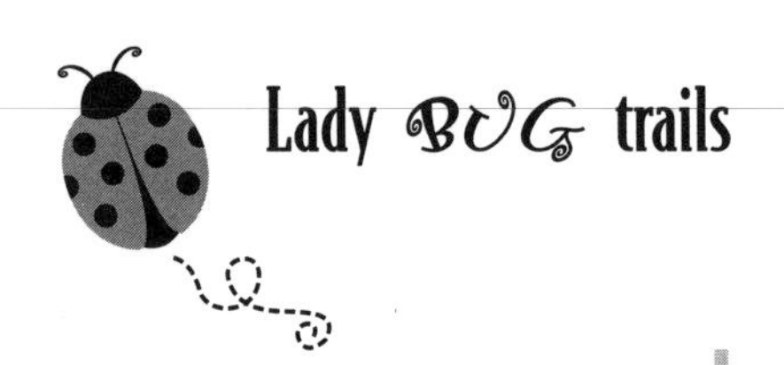

two scriptures that mention seraphs with wings (Isaiah 6:2, 6). However, most references about angels appearing to people in the Bible don't mention wings or flying. I just think it's fun to think about Daniel watching Gabriel fly.

Anyhoo...let's rejoin Mary in Nazareth. Our text says God sent the angel Gabriel to Nazareth, a town in Galilee (Luke 1:26). According to the *Holman Bible Dictionary*, Nazareth means "branch." It does not appear in the Old Testament. This was the hometown of Jesus. He became known as "Jesus of Nazareth." (See Matthew 26:71; Luke 18:37; 24:19; John 1:45; Acts 2:22; 3:6; 10:38.) Nazareth was located in lower Galilee about halfway between the Sea of Galilee and the Mediterranean Sea. It lay in the hill country. It was a small village in Jesus' day, having only one spring to supply fresh water. Today the spring is referred to as "Mary's well." Jesus grew from boyhood to manhood here (Luke 2:39-40; 4:16), being stamped as a Nazarene (Matthew 2:23). [6]

Did Nazareth have a good reputation? See John 1:46.

____

Luke 1:27 tells us that Mary was a virgin "pledged to be married" to a man named Joseph, a descendant of David. In today's vernacular we might say that Mary was engaged to Joseph. We would call her his fiancée. Their engagement period was much more binding in Bible times than it is today. To end a betrothal required a divorce, even though there were no sexual relations during this time. Loyalty was required. (I bet they didn't have many Runaway Brides!) Holman defines betrothal as "the act of engagement for marriage in Bible times and was as binding as marriage. Mary and Joseph were betrothed but did not live together. When Mary came to be with child during betrothal, Joseph decided to quietly divorce her." [7] (Of course, the angel changed Joseph's mind!)

Read Matthew 1:18-25. Notice that Matthew refers to Joseph and Mary as "husband" (v. 19) and "wife" (v. 24) **before** they were married. Again, times were different in those days. Write Matthew 1:25 on the lines below.

____

____

I take my hat off to Joseph. Verse 19 says he was a "righteous man" and did not want to expose Mary to public disgrace. This was even BEFORE the angel explained things to him. Read Matthew 1:24. What did Joseph do as soon as he woke up from his dream?

____

____

He did this, seemingly, without skipping a beat! Do you find that flabbergasting? I do. I am amazed at his faith. Notice what Joseph does not say? He does not say, "How can I be sure of this?" like somebody else we know! (See Luke 1:18). We will venture down that path tomorrow. For now, I'd like to close our time together with Gabriel's beautiful greeting to Mary. Read Luke 1:28 and write it on the lines below.

Drink those last five words into your soul. **The Lord is with you!** Believe it, Lady BUG Sisters! As the Lord was with Mary, so He is with us, too! Pour out your heart in praise for this wonderful truth. Do you have questions about something you read today? Write 'em down! Dig in the Word for the answers! Remember, there's no such thing as too many questions!☺

Day 2: Do Not Be Afraid

Snack to nibble on: Luke 1:37 For nothing is impossible with God!

Yesterday we left Gabriel and Mary in Nazareth. Let's join them there now. **Read Luke 1:28-38.**

Gabriel has just delivered the beautiful words, "Greetings, you who are highly favored! The Lord is with you." Notice Mary's reaction. Verse 29 says she was "greatly troubled" at his words and wondered what kind of greeting this might be!

Why do you think Mary was "greatly troubled" at his words?

____

____

The text tells us that Mary wondered about the greeting. I wondered, too, so I looked up the word "greetings" in my Greek dictionary. The original Greek word for "Greetings" in this context is *chairo*, which means "to rejoice, be glad, delighted; (as a greeting) Hail! [8] So...I'm sitting here thinking Gabriel tossed the first Hail Mary pass! Ha. ☺ "Greetings" in the Latin Vulgate is *Ave* (which is where we get Ave Maria!) [9] You may now proceed to sing or hum that song the rest of the day!

Notice the FIRST thing Gabriel says to Mary in verse 30.

"_ _ _ _ _ _ _ _ _ _ _ _ _!"

Now, let's rewind a bit to visit Zechariah in Luke 1:11-12. When the angel of the Lord appeared to Zechariah, what was his initial reaction? (v. 12) Circle all that apply.

He laughed.
He was startled.
He was gripped with fear.
He ignored the angel.

What did the angel say to him in verse 13?

"_ _ _ _ _ _ _ _ _ _ _ _ _!"

Sound familiar? This phrase **"Do not [or don't] be afraid!"** is used 89 times in the NIV Bible. This piqued my interest so I took a Lady BUG trail visiting these passages. You might want to do the same! I was thrilled to find out that our buddy Moses says it eleven times in Exodus and Deuteronomy! (Go, Mo, Go!) Joshua and Caleb, Samuel, David, Hezekiah, Isaiah, Joseph, Boaz, Jonathan, King Saul, Elijah, and Nehemiah used this phrase to encourage others. Jesus Himself was fond of making this powerful statement. (I counted 17 times!)

Read Luke 1:18 carefully. What question did Zechariah ask the angel?

____

____

Obviously, Zechariah was found lacking in the faith department. According to verse 20, what was his consequence for not believing the angel's words?

____

____

This seems rather harsh to me! After all, wasn't he just asking for a sign? Other Bible heroes asked for signs and weren't zapped with a MUTE button!

Read Genesis 15:8. Who asks the LORD, "How can I know that I will gain possession of the land?"

____

Read Judges 6: 14-18. Who asks for a sign? Why does he ask for this sign?

____

____

Read Judges 6:36-40. Describe what Gideon asks for. Summarize the story in your own words.

____

____

____

____

Do you ever get the hankering to scream out to God, **"Give me a sign!"** I have certainly had times in my life when I was just aching to squeeze the fleece and wring out the dew – desperate for a bowlful of water! Perhaps you have placed your own fleece before God? What happened? Use the Lady BUG trails margin.

Like Zech, do you ever want to ask the big question, "How can I be sure?"

I've wrestled with this concept. Why is it ok for Abram and Gideon to ask, "How can I know..." and "Give me a sign..." and it's not ok for Zechariah to ask, "How can I be sure?" In your opinion, what is the difference?

Perhaps the answer can be found in the following passage.

Genesis 15:6 states Abram "believed" the Lord would give him an heir, and his belief was credited to him as righteousness. Abram,
then in verse 8 asked how he could KNOW that he would gain possession of the land? God does not seem perturbed at Abram at all. Perhaps this is because God knew that Abram's questions were not based on a lack of faith! Read the following passage with your highlighter handy!

> Romans 4:18-25 (NIV) 18 **Against all hope, Abraham in hope believed** and so became the father of many nations, just as it had been said to him, "So shall your offspring be." 19 **Without weakening in his faith,** he faced the fact that his body was as good as dead—since he was about a hundred years old—and that Sarah's womb was also dead. 20 Yet **he did not waver through unbelief** regarding the promise of God, but was strengthened in his faith and gave glory to God, 21 **being fully persuaded that God had power to do what he had promised.** 22 This is why "it was credited to him as righteousness." 23 The words "it was credited to him" were written not for him alone, 24 but **also for us**, to whom God will credit righteousness—for us who believe in him who raised Jesus our Lord from the dead. 25 He was delivered over to death for our sins and was raised to life for our justification.

Against all hope, Abraham in hope believed! What does that mean to you?

Verses 23 and 24 make my heart skip a beat! I especially love that little phrase in verse 24 "but also for us!" Does that send chills down your spine or what? Summarize these two verses. How does that truth impact your life?

Let's make this personal. Here's what God wants from you and me. He wants us to:

Believe against all hope!
Face the facts without wavering in our faith.
Be strengthened in our faith.
Give Him the glory!
KNOW He has the power to fulfill His promises!

Here's the bottom line. He wants us to BELIEVE Him! Our belief will then be credited to us as righteousness! Close with a prayer telling God what you BELIEVE about Him!

Lady BUG trails

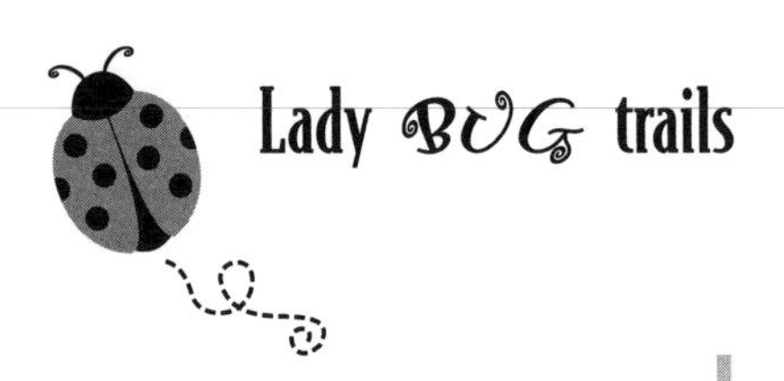

Day 3: Living the Lyrics: Voice of Truth

Our song for today is one of my favorite songs of all time. Why? Because it speaks to the heart of where I live! Soooooooooooooo many voices. Sooooooooooooooooooo many choices. As I said in the introduction of this Bible study, I believe that life, in a nutshell, is all about Voices and Choices! Our destiny is ultimately determined by the voices we listen to and the choices we make!

This powerful song reminds us of two great Bible stories. Likely, you've heard these stories many times before. As you read them today, jot down details that catch your eye. Answer the thought questions: Who, What, When, Where, Why, How? Involve yourself in the story as if you are an eyewitness to these events.

A Walk on the Waves! Read Matthew 14:22-33.

____

____

____

____

____

____

A Sling and a Stone! Read 1 Samuel 17:32-50.

____

____

____

____

____

____

Now, sing the song and meditate on the lyrics.

Voice of Truth

(Lyrics & Music: Mark Hall & Steven Curtis Chapman)

Oh what I would do to have
The kind of faith it takes to climb out of this boat I'm in
Onto the crashing waves

To step out of my comfort zone
Into the realm of the unknown where Jesus is
And He's holding out His hand

But the waves are calling out my name and they laugh at me
Reminding me of all the times I've tried before and failed
The waves they keep on telling me time and time again,
"Boy, you'll never win! You'll never win!"

Chorus:
But the Voice of Truth tells me a different story
The Voice of Truth says, "Do not be afraid!"
And the Voice of Truth says, "This is for My glory"
Out of all the voices calling out to me
I will choose to listen and believe the Voice of Truth

Oh what I would do to have
The kind of strength it takes to stand before a giant
With just a sling and a stone
Surrounded by the sound of a thousand warriors
Shaking in their armor
Wishing they'd have had the strength to stand

But the giant's calling out my name and he laughs at me
Reminding me of all the times I've tried before and failed
The giant keeps on telling me time and time again,
"Boy, you'll never win! You'll never win!"

But the stone was just the right size
To put the giant on the ground
And the waves they don't seem so high
From on top of them lookin' down
I will soar with the wings of eagles
When I stop and listen to the sound of Jesus
Singing over me

I will listen and believe
I will listen and believe the Voice of Truth
I will listen and believe, cause Jesus You are the Voice of Truth
And I will listen to You, You are...

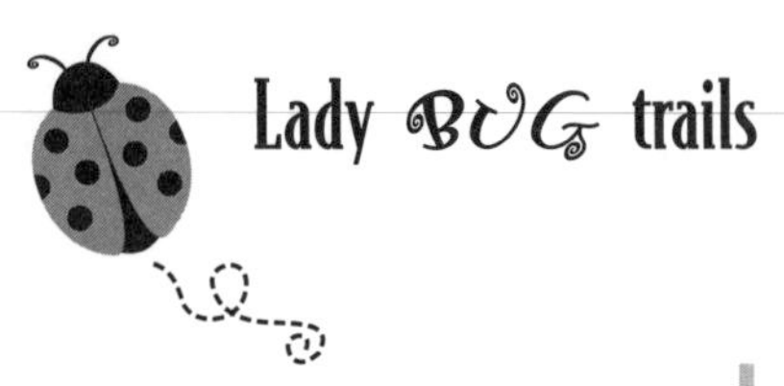

Can you relate to this song? What is your favorite verse? Why?

What does it take for you to step out of your comfort zone?

Close your eyes and sit back and relax. Take a deep breath or two. Consider those WAVES in the song. Do you have WAVES in your life calling out your name? Are your WAVES laughing at you? Are they reminding you of failures? Are your WAVES causing you to doubt your abilities? Are you making yourself seasick listening to their voices? Take some time to answer these questions. Reflection is good for the soul!

God's voice is telling quite another story. BE STILL AND KNOW THAT HE IS GOD! (Psalm 46:10) Allow His voice to tell you the truth about your situation. Record what you hear His voice saying to you.

Consider Goliath. The Bible tells us this "champion" was over nine feet tall! (1 Samuel 17:4) I wonder about the "champions" in our world today. You know, those larger-than-life giants towering over us with booming VOICES that shout, "You're not good enough!"

Do you have a Goliath in your mind? What does he tell you?

Again, allow the Voice of Truth to massage your heart. Write what you KNOW He wants you to hear today.

There are 2 crucial steps involved. We must:

Choose to listen to the Voice of Truth. AND...
Choose to believe the Voice of Truth.

Read John 18:37. Why did Jesus come into the world? What does everyone on the side of truth do?

Listen to the remarks Moses made to the Israelites. It is still a perfect message for us today! Consider his words:

> Now **choose life**, so that you and your children may live and that you may **love the LORD your God**, **listen to his voice**, and **hold fast to him.** For the LORD is your life, and he will give you many years in the land he swore to give to your fathers, Abraham, Isaac and Jacob. (Deuteronomy 30:19-21)

Read Isaiah 40:31. Find the line in the song that matches this verse and highlight it!

Write Zephaniah 3:17. Find the line in the song that matches this verse, highlight it, and then claim this TRUTH for your very own!

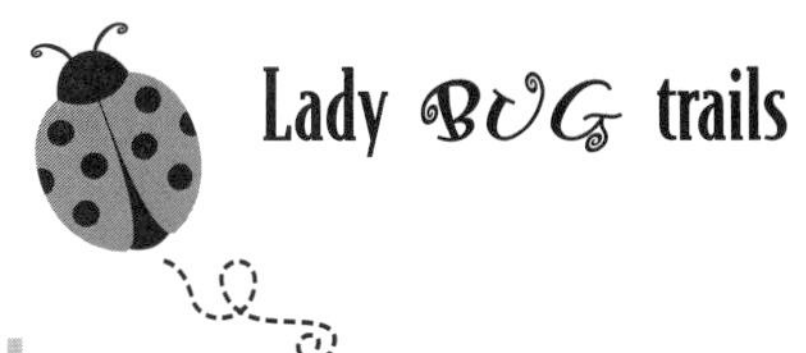

Day 4: How Can I Be Sure?

Snack to nibble on: Luke 1:18 "How can I be sure of this?"

Read Luke 1:1-25.

Let's take out our magnifying glasses and meticulously examine Zechariah's situation. We know he was a priest (v. 5). He was upright in the sight of God and observed all the Lord's commandments and regulations blamelessly (v. 6). He was chosen by lot to go into the temple of the Lord to burn incense (v. 9). I think it's fascinating that the angel appeared to him at the altar of incense. If you want to learn some interesting facts about the altar of incense read Exodus 30:1-10.

What interesting facts about the altar would you like to remember? If you're a visual learner you might even enjoy drawing the altar and labeling its parts. (I'll give you some extra space below.)

Incense was very symbolic in those days. Its fragrant smoke symbolized the prayers of God's people. (See Psalm 141:2; Revelation 5:8 and Revelation 8:3-4 if you'd like to take a Lady BUG Trail down Incense Lane!)

Here is Zechariah in the right place at the right time doing all the right things. But, according to Gabriel there's one enormous problem. Zechariah didn't BELIEVE God's words — the "good news!" (See Luke 1:19-20.)

Are we often guilty of doing the same thing today? We observe all the commands and regulations "blamelessly." We perform our duties at church. We offer prayers. We sing. We give cheerfully to the work of the church.
But...when it comes down to the nitty gritty do we really and truly with all of our hearts **BELIEVE** God? Do we take Him at His Word? Explore this idea honestly.

Sometimes we might feel like the boy's father in Mark 9:14-29. What did Jesus tell the boy's father in verse 23?

Notice v. 24. The boy's father IMMEDIATELY exclaimed,

"I do believe; help me overcome my unbelief!"

Do you feel his urgency? Do you see his transparency? Do you hear his honesty? Ever been there? How does this honest testimony speak to your heart?

Let's traipse back over to Mary's encounter with Gabriel. Zero in on Luke 1:34. Write Mary's question here.

Lady BUG trails

Compare Mary's question to the one that Zechariah asked in Luke 1:18. What are the similarities? What are the differences?

____

____

____

____

____

____

Zechariah and his wife were OLD! Mary was a virgin! Babies are not conceived every day in either of these two scenarios. Zech was reprimanded and "muted" for his question. Mary's question was answered with no consequence. Tell me why, tell me why?

____

____

____

____

If your answer includes the word "belief or unbelief" then you and I are on the same page! Don't you just love Luke 1:37? Write it here in big, bold letters!!!

_ _ _   _ _ _ _ _ _ _ _ _   _ _

_ _ _ _ _ _ _ _ _ _ _ _ _ _ _   _ _ _ _ _   _ _ _!

Focus on Mary's answer in verse 38.

"I am the Lord's servant.
May it be to me as you have said."

Oh...that we would reach down into the depths of our hearts and find that kind of faith!!! This week when you find yourself asking, "How can I be sure?" Remind yourself of this great scripture. Write Mark 9:23.

____

____

____

____

I just can't wait to DEVOUR Luke 1:45. It sums up the difference between Zechariah and Mary. It can serve as an inspiration for us the rest of our lives! We'll return to this passage later and hear it from Elizabeth's lips. For now, just allow these words to fall fresh on your ears.

Luke 1:45 Blessed is she who has <u>believed</u> that what the Lord has said to her will be accomplished!

Does this speak to your heart? How can you apply this truth to your current situation?

____

____

____

____

____

____

____

____

____

Do not be afraid!

[1] Seagraves
[2] Hail Mary pass
[3] Virgin Mary grilled cheese
[4] NIV Study Bible
[5] Zodhiates
[6] Butler
[7] Ibid
[8] Goodrick
[9] NIV Study Bible

Chapter 6:

The Original Lady BUG Savors the Favor!

Day 1: Highly Favored

Snack to nibble on: Luke 1:30-31 (NIV) Mary, you have found FAVOR with God. You will be with child and give birth to a son, and you are to give him the name Jesus.

Favor. A five-letter word with more than five different meanings! I asked our three children to tell me the first thing that popped into their heads when I said the word "favor."

Robert, our fifteen-year-old son said, "Something that one person does for another."

Jenny, our eleven-year-old daughter said, "Favor means choosing a favorite like, I favor mint chocolate chip ice cream more than plain chocolate ice cream."

Alli, our seven-year-old daughter said, "Favor is a doing word like when you ask me to do you a favor and sort the laundry."

Jot down your first thoughts about the word favor in the Lady BUG trails margin.

Frankly, my first thought was **"party favor"** probably because over the years my three kids have given and received about a trillion trinkets as parting gifts at a party!

Just for fun, let's look at a few definitions for the word favor from the *American Heritage Dictionary.*

fa·vor (fvr) *n.*
A gracious, friendly, or obliging act that is freely granted: *do someone a favor.*

Friendly or favorable regard; approval or support: *won the favor of the*

monarch; looked with favor on the plan.
A state of being held in such regard: *a style currently in favor.*
Unfair partiality; favoritism.

Something given as a token of love, affection, or remembrance.
A small decorative gift given to each guest at a party.
Advantage; benefit: *sailed under favor of cloudless skies.*
Behalf; interest: *an error in our favor.* [1]

So, this is how we define "favor" today. Let's travel back in time and eavesdrop on Gabriel and Mary's conversation. Listen carefully for the word "favor" and pay attention to how it is used in context.

Read **Luke 1:26-30**. Last week, we examined the phrase "Do not be afraid." Today, let's begin with the next power-packed phrase! Write it here. Luke 1:30b

"Mary, you have found ____________________ with God!"

Slide your feet into Mary's sandals. What was she feeling? What do you think this statement meant to her?

____

____

____

The original Greek word used in this context is *charis. Vine's Dictionary* says *charis* denotes (a) objectively, "grace in a person, graciousness," (b) subjectively, (1) "grace on the part of a giver, favor, kindness," (2) "a sense of favor received, thanks." [2]

I love the Amplified Bible's rendering of Luke 1:30

> *And the angel said to her, "Do not be afraid, Mary, for you have found grace (free, spontaneous, absolute favor and loving-kindness) with God!" Luke 1:30 (AMP)*

What could be better than that? Free! Spontaneous! Absolute favor! Loving-kindness! All rolled up into one beautiful package called GRACE! What does this word GRACE say to your heart? How is it free?

____

____

____

Notice that Gabriel had already told Mary that she's "highly favored" (v. 28). At first glance, I wondered if Gabriel was being a bit redundant by telling her again "you have found favor with God." But, then I found a nugget of truth in *The Complete Word Study Dictionary* that blew my doors off so I must share it with you!

The original Greek word for "highly favored" in verse 28 is not *charis*, but rather, *charitoo*. It is only used two times in the whole Bible. It means, "to grace, highly honor or greatly favor. In the NT spoken only of the divine favor, as to the Virgin Mary. It declares her to be highly favored, approved of God to conceive the Son of God through the Holy Spirit. The only other use of charitoo is in Eph. 1:6." [3]

Read Ephesians 1:1-8 (NIV).

> *[1] Paul, an apostle of Christ Jesus by the will of God, to the saints in Ephesus, the faithful in Christ Jesus: [2] **Grace (charis)** and peace to you from God our Father and the Lord Jesus Christ. [3] Praise be to the God and Father of our Lord Jesus Christ, who has blessed us in the heavenly realms with every spiritual blessing in Christ. [4] For he chose us in him before the creation of the world to be holy and blameless in his sight. In love [5] he predestined us to be adopted as his sons through Jesus Christ, in accordance with his pleasure and will— [6] to the praise of his glorious **grace [charis]** which he has **freely given [charitoo]** us in the One he loves. [7] In him we have redemption through his blood, the forgiveness of sins, in accordance with the riches of God's **grace [charis]** [8] that he lavished on us with all wisdom and understanding.*

What powerful message do you hear about *charis* and *charitoo*?

____

____

God deserves our praise! He has blessed us far more than we can ever deserve! Long before He spoke the world into existence He chose us to be His adopted daughters!

He has freely given us His GRACE (the ultimate party favor!) in Christ. We are "highly honored" and "greatly favored" to have redemption through Christ's blood. Can we even fathom the riches of His grace that He lavished (and continues to lavish) on us? I adore the word lavish! A synonym for lavish is extravagant! When you hear the word extravagant what comes to mind?

____

____

Lady BUG trails

The original Greek word for lavish is *perisseuo* which means "to have abundance, more than enough, overflow, to have an excessive amount of something, ranging from moderate excess to a very great degree of excess!" [4]

Stop and put your pen down. Close your Bible. Close your eyes. Stretch a blank canvas across your mind. Now, choose your medium: watercolors, acrylics, tempera, crayons, colored pencils, markers, chalk, or perhaps you want to go for the air brush! There are no rules. No directions. (No assembly required!) This art project will be created in your mind. No worries, you can't do it wrong! Your assignment is to illustrate God's extravagant grace. Consider how He has lavished His grace on you or a family member. Pray while you "paint" the masterpiece in your mind.

When you are finished record how you feel. What is ONE THING you better understand about God's grace?

____

____

____

____

____

____

____

____

____

____

____

____

Day 2: How Will This Be?

Snack to nibble on: Luke 1:34 "How will this be?"

Today we are going to carefully examine the rest of Gabriel's message to Mary. One big bombshell! Imagine being told all of this at one time.

Luke 1:31-33

You will be with child.
You will give birth to a son.
You are to give him the name Jesus.
He will be great and will be called the Son of the Most High.
God will give him David's throne.
Your son will reign over the house of Jacob forever!
Your son's kingdom will never end!

Now, slip into Mary's sandals again. Do you feel your knees wobblin'? Perhaps we have become so familiar with this story that we forget how ENORMOUS these declarations must have been for Mary. Which of these statements would have been hardest to "swallow" and why?

____

____

____

____

____

____

____

____

____

____

I wish the Bible specifically stated how old Mary was when she received this news. It does not! Scholars and historians and commentators all "guesstimate." Some say she was probably 13 because of the betrothal traditions of that day. Others say she "had to be" closer to 15. I read an article today that stated she "must have been" 20 or older. HUH? Who's right? Unfortunately, we will never know for sure. I wonder why we are specifically told the ages of others in the Bible.

Lady BUG trails

Read Genesis 5:21. How old was Enoch when he became the father of Methuselah? ______________________________

Read Genesis 17:17 and Genesis 21:5. How old were Abraham and Sarah when they had Isaac? ______________________________

Take a peek at Genesis 5:3. How old was Adam when he had Seth?

____

When did Noah become the father of Shem, Ham, and Japheth? (See Genesis 5:32.)

____

So...why aren't we told how old Mary was? Take a wild guess.

____

____

____

Your guess is as good as mine! There are some questions that just don't have answers. Surely God would have mentioned that detail if He wanted us to know it! Let's not add to God's Word by making assumptions about facts that just aren't in there! Let's face the facts - or the lack thereof - and say, Hey, we don't know how old Mary was! Moving right along...

We do know that Mary was a virgin. Read Luke 1:34. "How will this be...since I am a virgin?" I love the way Gabriel answers her question. Fill in the blanks from Luke 1:35-37.

The ______________ ______________ will come upon you.

The power of the Most High will ______________________ you.

So the holy one to be born will be called the ______________ of ______________!

Can you imagine Mary's eyes being the size of saucers? If there were ever a time for a "Moses Moment" (Exodus 3:11) this would have been it! Mary could have said, "Who am I, that I should become the mother of the Son of God?" She could have made excuses. "Suppose...? What if...? I've never...!" She could have even begged, "O Lord, please send someone else to do it!"

Unlike Moses, Mary didn't need convincing. Unlike Zechariah, Mary didn't ask, "How can I be sure of this?" She embraced the opportunity to do something great for God! How can we put this into practice in our daily lives?

____

____

____

____

____

____

Gabriel tells Mary that her relative Elizabeth is going to have a child in her old age and that she's in her sixth month. He then reminds Mary that nothing is impossible with God!

Let's read Mary's response from the New King James Version of the Bible.

> *Luke 1:38 (NKJV) Then Mary said, "Behold the maidservant of the Lord! Let it be to me according to your word." And the angel departed from her.*

Does Mary's response inspire you? If so, how?

____

____

____

____

____

____

____

____

____

Let's look at the first statement in her response. "Behold, the maidservant of the Lord!"

The original Greek word for "maidservant" is *doule*. It means "bondservant. A female servant, a handmaid." [5] I feel like singing "Make Me A Servant, Lord, Make Me Like Mary!" She certainly had the heart of a servant and soon her Son would become the greatest "Servant" of all time!

Read the following passages. After reading each Scripture write down a truth about being a servant. Next to that truth, complete the following sentence:

In my life this TRUTH means...

Matthew 23:11-12

Mark 9:33-37

Mark 10:35-45

Luke 22:24-27

John 12:26

Acts 3:13

Acts 4:27, 30

Here's a bite of tasty trivia. Moses was called "servant of the Lord" at least 27 times throughout Scripture. God called David His servant (2 Samuel 3:18; Ezekiel 34:24 and many other times). Paul was referred to as a servant (Acts 16:17; Romans 1:1; 1 Corinthians 3:5; Philippians 1:1; Colossians 1:23; Titus 1:1)

Feel free to take a Lady BUG Trail down Servant Lane when you have a moment and look up all these verses. You will be enormously blessed!

Close by asking God to show you ONE special way you can serve Him today!

Lady BUG trails

Lady BUG trails

Day 3: According to Your Word

Snack to nibble on: Luke 1:38b (NKJV) Let it be to me according to your word!

For the sake of clarity, refresh your memory by reading Luke 1:26-38 again. (Be on the lookout for something new to jump off the page!)

Did you notice anything in the text that you'd like to study further? Write it down!

____

____

____

____

Yesterday we looked at Mary's response to Gabriel in the New King James Version. We discussed Mary's desire to be a servant. Here's the second statement in her response.

> *Luke 1:38 (NKJV) Then Mary said, "Behold the maidservant of the Lord! Let it be to me* ***according to your word."*** *And the angel departed from her.*

How would our lives change if we woke up every morning with Mary's words on our lips:

"Let it be to me according to your WORD!"

____

____

____

____

Psalm 119 – the longest chapter in the Bible – is a devotional on the word of God. Let the truth from each of these passages massage your soul! Personalize each one with YOUR name and use modern language. Consider each of these a "mini prayer" today!

Psalm 119:9

Psalm 119:25

Psalm 119:28

Psalm 119:37

Take a moment to consider those "worthless things" you want to turn your eyes away from. What do you WANT to feast your eyes on?

Psalm 119:65

Psalm 119:107

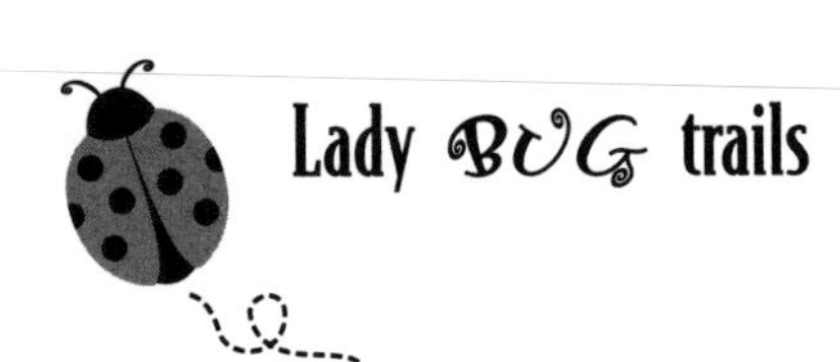

Psalm 119: 133

STOP THE PRESSES! HOLD THE PHONE! Ask yourself (and God) this very important, oh-so-intimate, life-altering question, "Is there a sin ruling over me?" Deal with this now. There's no time like the present!

Psalm 119:169 This sounds like a Lady BUG verse if I've ever heard one! **Ladies Better Understanding God** — that's who we want to be! Use the margin to write this verse in BOLD letters!

Let it be to me
According to His Word
I gratefully
Savor the favor!

Taste and see
That the Lord is good
His GRACE
Is a marvelous flavor!

-Denell Dennis

Day 4: Living the Lyrics: Amazing Grace

I've heard grace and mercy described in the following way:

"Grace is receiving what we do not deserve.
Mercy is not receiving what we deserve."

Do you agree or disagree with this definition? Recall a specific example in your own life when you received grace. Did you deserve it? How did you feel? Have you given or received mercy in a unique situation? Record the details here.

____

____

____

____

____

____

____

____

____

Our song for today beautifully describes God's grace to us. It has been called the world's "best-loved hymn." Most likely you've heard this song before, possibly dozens of times. You may even have it memorized. (I certainly do!) We know the song by its most famous title, "Amazing Grace," but this was not the original title. John Newton wrote this song in Olney, England probably in 1773 to accompany his New Year's sermon. It was published in Olney Hymns in 1779 under the heading ***Faith's Review and Expectation***, along with a reference to 1 Chronicles 17:16-17. [6]

Praise God for modern technology! Two hundred years ago the first edition of the Olney Hymns was published. Since that time many of the hymns have become well known wherever Christianity is practiced. In response to many requests the trustees of the Cowper and Newton Museum created a facsimile volume of the first edition. Because it's public domain I'm able to share it with you! [7] Please sing the hymn and FEAST upon every word.

Facsimile of Original, 1779

Hymn 41

John Newton

8,6,8,6

Faith's review and expectation.
1Chr 17:16,17

Amazing grace! (how sweet the sound)
That saved a wretch like me!
I once was lost, but now am found,
Was blind, but now I see.

'Twas grace that taught my heart to fear,
And grace my fears relieved;
How precious did that grace appear,
The hour I first believed!

Through many dangers, toils and snares,
I have already come;
'Tis grace has brought me safe thus far,
And grace will lead me home.

The LORD has promised good to me,
His word my hope secures;
He will my shield and portion be,
As long as life endures.

Yes, when this flesh and heart shall fail,
And mortal life shall cease,
I shall possess, within the veil,
A life of joy and peace.

The earth shall soon dissolve like snow,
The sun forbear to shine;
But GOD, who called me here below,
Will be for ever mine.

I've got chills. They're multiplyin'! Feasting my eyes on a facsimile of the original hymn stirs up all kinds of nostalgia. What questions, comments, responses, or observations come to your mind about this hymn?

____

____

My poet eyeballs popped right out of their sockets when I read the 8,6,8,6 notation. In case you're curious, these numbers explain the meter of the hymn, which is synonymous with the number of syllables per line of poetry. Clap the syllables of each line and you will find the 8,6,8,6 pattern in every stanza! Eureka! I've never really looked at this song in its poetry form before. How refreshing to learn something new about something so very old! Now, let's take a peek at the title of this hymn. Write it here.

Faith's __________ and _______________.

At first glance, why do you think John Newton chose this title?

____

____

To help us dip our quills into John's inkwell we need to know more about his life. John Newton was born in London in 1725. His father was a commander of a merchant ship that sailed the Mediterranean. His mother was a devoted, God-fearing woman who made it her goal in life to nurture John's soul. At his mother's knee, John memorized Bible passages and hymns. She prayed for him. She LOVED him. Although John's mother died before he was 7 years old, her influence stayed with him throughout his lifetime. What Scripture or Biblical principle does this bring to your mind?

____

____

You may have thought of many others. This is the Scripture that came to my mind. Write Proverbs 22:6.

____

____

John Newton is a case in point for this proverb. He memorized Scripture at an early age and was trained by a devoted mother. After her death, John chose to "make waves" on the high seas. At age 11 he began taking voyages with his father. Later, at age 19, he was forced into service with the British Navy. John was miserable so he deserted the navy and was later captured. I

wonder while he was being publicly FLOGGED for misconduct if memories of his mother's teaching burned in his soul! John went through many more "dangers, toils and snares"! Listen to the words he spoke about himself, "I was very wicked, and therefore very foolish; and being my own enemy, I seemed determined that nobody should be my friend." [8] Can you think of a Scripture that would have been applicable to his situation? Write it here.

____

____

Some say John Newton had a reputation for profanity, coarseness, and "debauchery" (extreme indulgence in sensual pleasures) [9] which even shocked some of the sailors! He was known as "The Great Blasphemer." [10] One stormy night in March of 1748 John's ship was attacked by a brutal storm. In his desperation he cried out to God. Later, in his journal John wrote, "on that day the Lord sent from on high and delivered me out of deep waters." [11] This brings to mind a beautiful passage of praise written by the psalmist, David. Read 2 Samuel 22:1-20. Write verse 17 in the Lady BUG trails margin. Glance back at verse 20. Why did God rescue David?

____

____

Woo Hoo! What a thrill to know that God rescues us because He delights in us! Even when we don't deserve it, He delights in us!

I wish I could tell you that John Newton jumped ship a new Christian man, freed all the slaves, and lived happily ever after! But, like us — and like the psalmist David — John's life was filled with proud moments and not-so-proud moments. He continued making his living in the slave trade. Some say he saw to it that the slaves under his care were treated humanely, though. [12] He met and married the love of his life, Mary.

According to Barbara Mikkelson, John Newton "eventually grew into his conversion, so that by the end of his days he actually was the godly man one would expect to have penned 'Amazing Grace'. But it was a slow process effected over the passage of decades, not something that happened with a clap of thunder and a flash of lightning. In Newton's case, the 'amazing grace' he wrote of might well have referred to God's unending patience with him." [13]

What is your heart's reaction to this? Can you relate? Have you "grown into" your conversion, too? Are you still a work in progress like me? No Rules...Just Write.

____

____

____

Sixteen years after his "Come to Jesus Meeting" on the sea, John Newton began his ministry preaching in Olney, England. In January 1773, he preached on 1 Chronicles 17:16-17 and presumably wrote the song, "Faith's Review and Expectation," to accompany his sermon. Fascinated by this fun fact, I immediately grabbed my Bible to look up the Scriptures. Then, it occurred to me that John Newton would have been reading from the King James Version of the Bible. Knowing what we now know about John Newton's past, let's read through his spectacles and attempt to feel what he felt more than 200 years ago. Please read the passage with a highlighter in hand in case a phrase JUMPS off the page! ☺

> ***1 Chronicles 17:16-17 (King James Version)*** *[16] And David the king came and sat before the LORD, and said, "Who am I, O LORD God, and what is mine house, that thou hast brought me hitherto? [17] And yet this was a small thing in thine eyes, O God; for thou hast also spoken of thy servant's house for a great while to come, and hast regarded me according to the estate of a man of high degree, O LORD God."*

Eureka! What 3 little words did King David utter that sound a bit like a Moses Moment?

___ ___ ___   ___ ___   ___

What is the difference between King David's "Who Am I" scenario and the "Who Am I" burning bush Moses moment? Do you hear a different attitude? Is there a different motivation or frame of mind? (Refresh your memory with Exodus 3:11, if you need to.)

____

____

____

____

Lady BUG trails

I would like to suggest that the beloved hymn, later called "Amazing Grace," was born to John Newton during his own Who Am I moment! In fact, if you would like to see Newton's actual "sermon notes" from January 1, 1773, you can access that information through The John Newton Project on the web. [14] Let's close our time together looking back at the song. These are the six original stanzas. (Others were added later.) Highlight or circle your favorite stanza. Re-write it in your own words as a declaration of your life thus far.

____

____

____

____

John Newton lived to be eighty-two years old. He wrote, "My memory is nearly gone; but I remember two things: that I am a great sinner, and that Christ is a great Savior." [15] He continued to preach up until the last year of his life, although he was blind by that time. Perhaps John Newton shared JC Penney's view of blindness, "My eyesight may be getting weaker, but my vision is increasing." [16]

---

1 favor
2 Vine
3 Zodhiates
4 Goodrick
5 Zodhiates
6 Rogers
7 Newton
8 The John Newton Project
9 Morris
10 John Newton – The Reformed Reader
11 Ibid
12 Rogers
13 Mikkelson
14 The John Newton Project
15 John Newton – The Reformed Reader
16 Max Lucado

Chapter 7:

The Original Lady BUG's Bundle of Joy

Day 1: Great Things

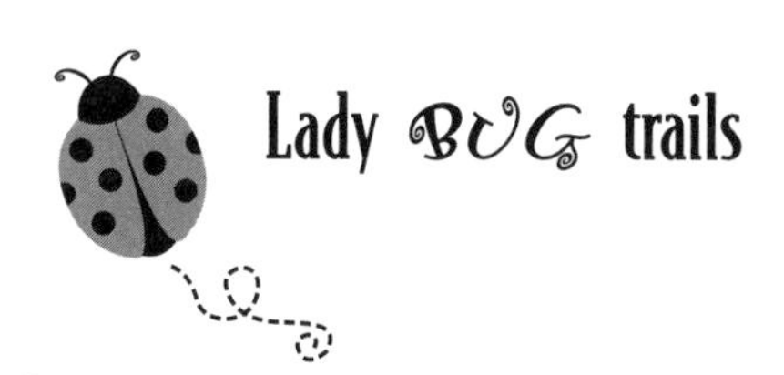

Snack to nibble on: Luke 1:49 "The Mighty One has done great things for me - holy is His name!"

Read Luke 1:39-45.

Verse 39 says, "At that time...." Rewind to verse 38 to see Gabriel had just left Mary. Imagine how she must have been feeling! So much to take in. So many emotions! Contemplate what may have been going through her mind as she packed her bags to visit Elizabeth. Think back to a time in your own life when you received some startling, mind-boggling, life-altering news. (Good news or bad news.) In either case, after this pivotal news you knew your life would never be the same. What were your emotions? What did you do first? Did you share this news with anyone? If so, who?

____

____

I'm not surprised that Mary "**hurried**" to see her relative Elizabeth. I would have been in a hurry, too! She must have been bursting at the seams with excitement. I wish we had a few more details about their first few moments together. Verse 41 says, "When Elizabeth heard Mary's greeting...." I want to know how Mary greeted her! What did she say? Did she ***run*** into their home? Did she jump up and down? Did she bow low to the ground? Did she call her by name? Did she pat Elizabeth's tummy?

What look was on Elizabeth's face when baby John leaped for joy in her womb? This was NOT a "Braxton Hicks" moment. This was a supernatural, larger-than-life moment! This was not just a good thing, but a God Thing! I wonder if this was the exact time that the prophecy in Luke 1:15 was fulfilled.

Read Luke 1:15. Write the last part of verse 15.

____

Were mother and babe filled with the Holy Spirit simultaneously? Notice after Elizabeth was filled with the Holy Spirit she didn't just talk to Mary, she exclaimed in a loud voice!

Blessed are you among women!
Blessed is the child you will bear!

Study Elizabeth's question in verse 43. (Is this a Moses Moment or not?) Instead of saying, "Who am I...?" she says, "Why am I...?" In your own words, what was Elizabeth essentially saying?

____

____

Elizabeth had been barren her whole life and now, in her old age, was six months pregnant! She had already been feeling God's "favor" because of what the Lord had specifically done for her. Read Luke 1:25.

What had God shown and what had He taken away?

____

Now, she's feeling "SO favored" because Mary, the mother of her Lord, had come to her. Luke 1:24 tells us that Elizabeth had been in "seclusion" for five months. Whoa! That's a long time! It must have been a breath of fresh air for Elizabeth to have a visitor. And, not just any run-of-the-mill visitor either. This visitor would soon give birth to God!

Here's a question. Why had Elizabeth been in seclusion for five months? Various commentators speculate modesty, humility, devotion toward God, joy. Some say it was to avoid rumors. What do you think?

____

____

Luke 1:25 is crucial. Write Elizabeth's statement and place a big exclamation point at the end!

____

____

We've already discussed Luke 1:45 but let's look at it again imagining the scene. Picture Elizabeth, "well along in years," belly protruding, face glowing, filled with the Holy Spirit. Was she holding Mary's hand? Were tears of joy streaming down both of their faces?

Write Luke 1:45.

____

____

What a perfect time for Mary to break out in song! Read Luke 1:46-55 (NIV).

Taking a peek into the window of Mary's soul, here's the first thing I see. **HUMILITY!** This celebration song is all about GOD! Moments before, Elizabeth had just declared Mary to be "blessed among women." Elizabeth had placed Mary on a pedestal as the "mother of my Lord" questioning why she was even privileged enough to be in the same room with her! Mary, though, gives all the credit to God. Her soul glorifies the Lord. Her spirit rejoices in God. She calls God her "Savior." This is the first time the word "Savior" appears in the New Testament.

Take a closer look at Luke 1:48. Mary is rejoicing that her Savior has been mindful of her "humble" state. In verse 52 she rejoices that God has "lifted up the humble." How poetic and prophetic that years later Mary's Son would utter the words, "The greatest among you will be your servant!" (Matthew 23:11) Fill in the blanks from Matthew 23:12.

For whoever ___________himself will be humbled, and whoever

____________ himself will be ______________!

This causes me to break out in song in my own heart! If you know this song, sing along!

Humble yourselves in the sight of the Lord (echo)
Humble yourselves in the sight of the Lord (echo)
And He (and He) will lift (will lift) you up
And He (and He) will lift (will lift) you up!

Yes, it is scriptural for generations to call the Virgin Mary "blessed." We just need to remember the reason she was given that title. She knew it well. Look at verse 49, "The Mighty One has done great things for me - holy is HIS name!" Does His greatness overwhelm you like it does me? In Deuteronomy 11:7 Moses reminds his listeners "It was your own eyes that saw all these great things the LORD has done!" Let's ask God today to keep our eyes open to the great things He has already done and to eagerly look for the great things He has in store for us!

Lady BUG trails

Notice how Mary continues to make this song all about HIM in verses 50-55.

His mercy...He has performed...He has scattered...He has brought down and lifted up...He has filled and sent away...He has helped...remembering to be merciful!

I applaud Mary for her servant heart and her gratefulness to God. I wonder if she had requested to hear the story of Hannah over and over again at bedtime through the years. Read and compare. List similarities in the margin.

Hannah's Prayer: 1 Samuel 2:1-10

1 Then Hannah prayed and said:
"My heart rejoices in the LORD;
in the LORD my horn is lifted high.
My mouth boasts over my enemies,
for I delight in your deliverance.
2 "There is no one holy like the LORD;
there is no one besides you;
there is no Rock like our God.
:3 "Do not keep talking so proudly
or let your mouth speak such arrogance,
for the LORD is a God who knows,
and by him deeds are weighed.
4 "The bows of the warriors are broken,
but those who stumbled are armed with strength.
5 Those who were full hire themselves out for food,
but those who were hungry hunger no more.
She who was barren has borne seven children,
but she who has had many sons pines away.
6 "The LORD brings death and makes alive;
he brings down to the grave and raises up.
7 The LORD sends poverty and wealth;
he humbles and he exalts.
8 He raises the poor from the dust
and lifts the needy from the ash heap;
he seats them with princes
and has them inherit a throne of honor.
"For the foundations of the earth are the LORD's;
upon them he has set the world.
9 He will guard the feet of his saints,
but the wicked will be silenced in darkness.
"It is not by strength that one prevails;
10 those who oppose the LORD will be shattered.
He will thunder against them from heaven;
the LORD will judge the ends of the earth.
"He will give strength to his king
and exalt the horn of his anointed."

Mary's Song: Luke 1:46-55

46 And Mary said:
"My soul glorifies the Lord
47 and my spirit rejoices in God my Savior,
48 for he has been mindful
Of the humble state of his servant.
From now on all generations will call me blessed,
49 for the Mighty One has done great things for me—holy is his name.
50 His mercy extends to those who fear him,
From generation to generation.
51 He has performed mighty deeds with his arm;
He has scattered those who are proud in their inmost thoughts.
52 He has brought down rulers from their thrones
But has lifted up the humble.
53 He has filled the hungry with good things
But has sent the rich away empty.
54 He has helped his servant Israel,
Remembering to be merciful
55 to Abraham and his descendants forever,
Even as he said to our fathers."

Highlight or circle verse 53 of Mary's song. "He has filled the hungry with good things!" Amen and Amen! Share your thoughts about this great passage.

Let's close our time today by taking a moment to stop and smell the roses. The Mighty One has done great things for us! So often we get consumed with the daily ho-hum. Let's take this moment to list some of the GREAT THINGS God has done. Not just good, but as Tony the Tiger would say, "They're Grrrreeeeeeaaaatt!" Think about your own personal situation. Resist the temptation to list what He's done for your husband, kids, parents, or friends. I want you to dig deep, uncover, rediscover, remember, and appreciate what He has done specifically for little ole' YOU!

Day 2: Living the Lyrics: Breath of Heaven

Luke 1:56 says "Mary stayed with Elizabeth for about three months and then returned home." The timing suggests that Mary may have stayed with Elizabeth until John was born. I am guessing Mary was a tremendous help to her physically and emotionally. In turn, Elizabeth must have been an enormous influence for Mary.

When I was pregnant with our first child, Robert, I devoured every page of *What To Expect When You're Expecting* wanting to be prepared in every way! [1] We took childbirth classes and decorated the nursery, etc. In fact, we were experiencing a "baby boom" at our church at that time so God provided me with more than a few opportunities to get the "scoop" from new mothers about the special delivery process.

If we had been ladybugs on the wall of Elizabeth's home, eavesdropping, what might we have overheard Mary and Elizabeth chatting about in the wee hours?

____

____

____

____

____

We will not take time to read every detail of the events surrounding John's birth in this study but you would certainly be blessed by reading the story. Luke 1:57-80. (His story makes a great Lady BUG trail!)

Mary's timeline is a bit fuzzy after she left Elizabeth's home. At some point, the Lord appeared to Joseph in a dream explaining the situation. Let's refresh our memories from the gospel of Matthew.

Read Matthew 1:18-25.

They lived together under the same roof but did not share the same bed. I am curious. What did they discuss at the dinner table? Did Joseph lovingly place his hand on Mary's swollen belly to feel the baby kick? Or, did he feel like a 3rd wheel? Did Mary send Joseph out for pickles and ice cream in the middle of the night? Ha. Mary must have been overwhelmed at times, especially when Joseph broke the news to her about having to hop on a donkey and make a 3-day trip from Nazareth to Bethlehem to register for the census.

Read Luke 2:1-7 slowly. Do your best to read it as if you've never heard it before. Make notes as you go. Is there something in the passage you've never noticed before?

___

___

___

___

___

___

___

___

___

___

___

___

The mother of Jesus Christ was a REAL woman. She was flesh and blood just like you and me! Imagine what she must have been feeling just before giving birth.

The author of our song today set her thoughts to music. Sing "Breath of Heaven, Mary's Song." Imagine being Mary. Feel what she felt. Allow the Breath of Heaven to hold you together while you sing! Use your creativity to illustrate this song any way you choose!

Lady BUG trails

Breath of Heaven, Mary's Song

(Written by Amy Grant and Chris Eaton)

I have traveled many moonless nights
Cold and weary, with a babe inside
And I wonder what I've done
Holy Father, you have come
And chosen me now to carry your son

I am waiting in a silent prayer
I am frightened by the load I bear
In a world as cold as stone,
Must I walk this path alone
Be with me now, be with me now

Chorus:
Breath of heaven
Hold me together
Be forever near me
Breath of heaven
Breath of heaven
Lighten my darkness
Pour over me your holiness
For you are holy
Breath of heaven

Do you wonder as you watch my face
If a wiser one should have had my place
But I offer all I am
For the mercy of your plan
Help me be strong
Help me be
Help me

What is your favorite part of the song? Why?

Go back and read what you just wrote. How will you LIVE those lyrics this week?

Perhaps today, you're waiting in a silent prayer. Are you frightened by the load you bear? If you're stumbling in the dark, ask Him to turn the Light on for you! Whatever the circumstance, give it to the Mighty One who has done and will do great things for you!

Day 3: Wonder of All Wonders

Snack to nibble on: Luke 2:7 Mary gave birth to her firstborn, a son. She wrapped him in cloths and placed him in a manger.

A dear friend recently gave me a bookmark. (Yes, it had ladybugs on it, in case you were wondering!) ☺ But, most of all, I love the scripture on the bookmark.

Stop and consider God's wonders! Job 37:14

As I begin writing today's lesson, I am overwhelmed with His wonders! I echo David's declaration in Psalm 40:5, "Our God has done MANY wonders... too many to declare!"

Read the 37th chapter of Job. Write Job 37:5 (NIV).

____

____

I ditto Elihu's sentiments in Job 37:1 ***"My heart pounds and leaps from its place!"*** God does great things beyond our understanding! As "Lady BUGs" (Ladies Better Understanding God) we want to understand Him better! And yet...we know it is impossible to ever understand everything about Him. Notice what these verses say about God's greatness.

Job 36:26 ______________________________________

Ps. 145:3 ______________________________________

It's so hard to fathom His majesty and His Almighty power. I like the word "fathom." It's kind of funky and FUN to say. There are two original Hebrew words for fathom in the Old Testament. The first one is *heqer*. It's a "masculine noun referring to a search, an inquiry, something to be searched out. The Lord's understanding is declared to be unsearchable, among other things. Used figuratively, it denotes the deep things or depths of God to be examined." [2]

Write these passages in your own words.

Isaiah 40:28

____

____

Job 5:9

____

____

Job 9:10

____

____

The other Hebrew word translated fathom is *masa*. It means to find out, discover, or uncover! [3] What is the main idea for each of these scriptures?

Job 11:7

____

____

Ecclesiastes 3:11

____

____

Today we will stop and consider God's wonders that surrounded the birth of Christ. We'll be camping out in Luke 2. Read Luke 2:1-7 out loud, if possible, listening for any GEM you might find along the way. If you made notes about this same passage on Day 2, review them now with new eyes! What fascinates you most? Record in the margin.

What a co-inky-dink (not!) that the census was to be taken at precisely this time in history. I stand in awe of the way God orchestrated every itty bitty piece of minutia to fulfill prophecy! Augustus means "exalted." [4] Woo Woo! A Big Wig, to be sure! Many scholars believe Caesar Augustus was the greatest Roman emperor of all time. He may have thought he was pretty hot stuff when he issued the decree for the census to be taken. A man with a plan! But, we know full well who was really behind the decision. Fill in the blanks. Proverbs 19:21 (NIV)

Many are the __________ in a man's heart, but it is the _________'s _______________ that prevails!

In this case, we can see the LORD'S purpose prevailing! It had been prophesied that Jesus would come out of Bethlehem, David's hometown. It had also been prophesied that Jesus would be a "Nazarene." How clever and creative our God is to work out all the details so He could be both! Read the following and take note of the key words!

Isaiah 11:1

Jeremiah 33:14-16

Micah 5:2

Matthew 2:4-6, 23

Luke 1:32-33

John 7:41-42

Following childbirth in biblical days there were certain customs. Ezekiel 16:4 gives us a general idea. John Gill gives us a little more history. On the day a child was born:

The cord was cut (usually by the midwife).
The baby was washed with water (usually hot) to cleanse it from blood and to make the skin soft.
The baby was rubbed with salt, either by sprinkling salt, or using salt and water, for cleanliness and to make the skin firm.
The baby was wrapped in cloths for warmth and security. [5]

As far as we know, there was no midwife or nurse at the birth so I'm guessing Mary or Joseph did the honors. I wonder what they used to cut Christ's cord! I wonder if they were able to find clean water to wash the baby with. Did they rub Him with salt? If so, had they packed it in anticipation of His arrival? We know they wrapped Him in cloths. As a child I heard the following verse in the King James Version:

And she brought forth her firstborn son, and wrapped him in swaddling clothes, and laid him in a manger; because there was no room for them in the inn. Luke 2:7 (KJV) I always wondered what swaddling clothes were. (Sounded more like clothes for a waddling duck than for a newborn baby!) ☺ The original Greek word used in this context is sparganoo, meaning a swaddling band "to wrap (in cloth); to bind a newborn infant in strips of long cloth, a normal act of child care for warmth, security, etc." [6]

This practice is in full swing even today! You can go online and order a Swaddle Me Adjustable Newborn Wrap [7] from the Internet. I kid you not! Times have certainly changed but the need for a newborn to be "swaddled" has not. I vividly remember standing in the hospital room fifteen years ago with my hubby on the day of our firstborn's birth. The nurse taught us how to properly "swaddle" him in his receiving/security blanket.

If you're a mother, you may have a remembrance of swaddling your firstborn. If so, jot down your memories. Be specific.

____

____

____

According to William Barclay, swaddling clothes in biblical days consisted of a square of cloth with a long, bandage-like strip coming diagonally off one corner. The child was first wrapped in the square of cloth, and then the long strip was wound round and round about him. [8] Now, imagine Mary doing this with her newborn Son! She must have been ever-so-careful to wrap Him just right! Not too loose, not too tight! Were Gabriel's words ringing in her ears as she placed Him in the manger?

Name him Jesus. He will be great...the Son of the Most High...he'll sit on David's throne...he'll reign over the house of Jacob forever...his kingdom will never end...he is the Holy One...he is the Son of God!

Gabriel didn't mention that the Son of the Most High would be sleeping in a feeding trough! Imagine how Mary's hands shook as she held Him for the first time. As she looked into His eyes, what did she see? How did she feel? I'm sad that we only have one verse and it's sparse. "She gave birth." I want to know how long she was in labor. Did she have pain or was she exempt? Did Joseph jokingly say, "It's a boy!" Did they weep? What questions or comments do you have?

____

____

The Greek word for manger is *phatne* which means a "manger or crib." In Luke 13:15 this word is rendered "stall." Some scholars believe Mary and Joseph stayed in a cave near the village. [9] Others believe they stayed in a stable, an open courtyard attached to the inn. The manger was most likely a feeding trough used for cattle, sheep, donkeys, or horses. [10] (I enjoy the imagery that sheep may have been fed there! Perhaps the Good Shepherd felt right at home from the start!) **Read Luke 2:8-20.**

How fitting that His first visitors were shepherds! Notice the first four words of the angel in Luke 2:10.

_ _   _ _ _   _ _   _ _ _ _ _ _ !

Perhaps, by now, we have this phrase memorized! *Do not be afraid, Moses! Do not be afraid, Zechariah! Do not be afraid, Mary! Do not be afraid, Joseph!*

Fear. Such a common reaction. What was the antidote for their fear? **Good News of Great Joy!** This is a lesson for us on those days when we are gripped with fear or uncertainty. There is good news of great joy for us, too! What is our "good news" and why would it cause us to have "great joy" as a Christian?

____

____

____

____

Read Acts 10:34-36. Peter says God told the "**good news of peace**" through Jesus.

PEACE, PERFECT PEACE! This leads us to the goosebumps part of Luke 2! Read Luke 2:13-14 imagining the scene. The angel declares peace on earth on the day the Prince of Peace is born!

Luke 2:14 is often called Gloria in Excelsis Deo, from the first words of the Latin Vulgate translation (meaning "Glory to God in the Highest"). [11] Feel free to hum that song for the rest of the day!

Day 4: Living the Lyrics: Mary, Did You Know?

During this time in the Roman world, the people were experiencing a time of "peace" called the Pax Romana (Roman Peace) under the rule of Caesar Augustus (see Luke 2:1). [12] The "peace" the angel declared was a different kind altogether! In your opinion, what is the difference between external peace and internal peace?

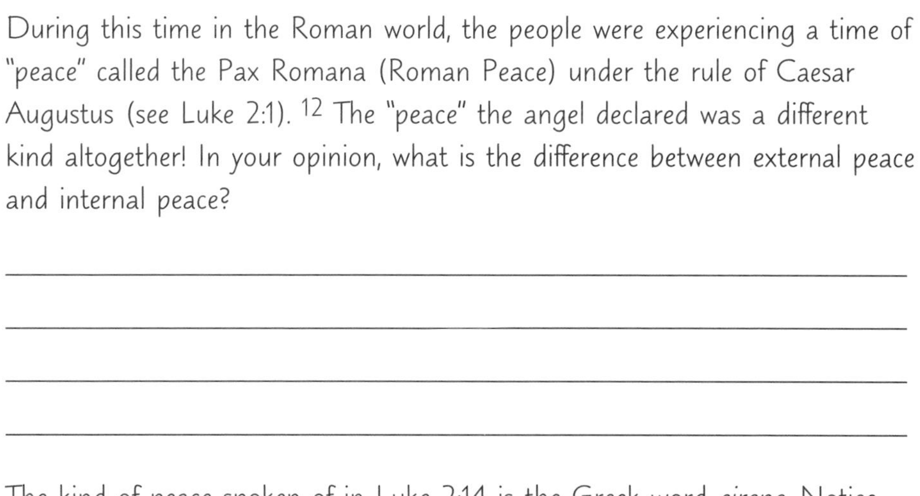

____

____

____

____

The kind of peace spoken of in Luke 2:14 is the Greek word *eirene*. Notice the English synonyms:

Peace
Harmony
Tranquility
Safety
Welfare
Health

Pay close attention to this definition. "**Eirene** is often used with an emphasis on lack of strife or reconciliation in a relation, as when one has 'peace with God'. It's often used as a verbal and written greeting. It generally follows the meanings and usage of the Hebrew word **salom** which means peace; having a focus of security; safety which can bring feelings of satisfaction, well-being, and contentment!" [13]

Luke 2:16 says the shepherds "hurried off" and found Mary, Joseph, and the baby (the Prince of Peace) lying in a manger. I can only imagine the stories they told Mary and Joseph! Talk about a Kodak moment! Did they all talk at once? How did they describe the glory of the Lord that had shone around them? Did they recount every detail of their praise and worship experience? Could they find the words to describe the great company of the heavenly host? How did the shepherds introduce themselves? Or, were they at a total loss for words when they feasted their eyes on the Savior of the world wrapped in swaddling clothes! Verse 17 says the shepherds "spread the word." All who heard the good news of great joy were amazed!

Now, let's focus on Luke 2:19. Take out your magnifying glass and examine this one closely! What did Mary do?

______________________________ up all these things.

______________________________ them in her heart.

Treasured and pondered. Two magnificent words! Mary was taking it all in, attempting to absorb the enormity of the situation.

I don't believe Mary KNEW the exact details of the future. But, I do think she believed now more than ever what Gabriel had told her. Nothing is impossible with God! (Luke 1:37)

Let's close our time together by singing "Mary, Did You Know?" Record every "treasure" you ponder in your heart.

____

____

____

____

____

____

____

____

____

____

____

____

____

Great are the works of the LORD; they are pondered by all who delight in them! Ps. 111:2

Mary, Did You Know?

(Written by Buddy Greene and Mark Lowry)

Mary, did you know
That your baby boy will one day walk on water?
Mary, did you know
That your baby boy will save our sons and daughters?
Did you know
That your baby boy has come to make you new?
This child that you've delivered
Will soon deliver you

Mary, did you know
That your baby boy will give sight to a blind man?
Mary, did you know
That your baby boy will calm a storm with his hand?
Did you know
That your baby boy has walked where angels trod?
And when you kiss your little baby
You've kissed the face of God

The blind will see
The deaf will hear
And the dead will live again
The lame will leap
The dumb will speak
The praises of the lamb

Mary, did you know
That your baby boy is Lord of all creation?
Mary, did you know
That your baby boy will one day rule the nations?
Did you know
That your baby boy is heaven's perfect lamb?
This sleeping child you're holding
Is the Great I AM!

[1] Eisenberg
[2] Baker
[3] Goodrick
[4] The NIV Study Bible
[5] Gill
[6] Goodrick
[7] Baby Universe
[8] Barclay, p. 16
[9] Zodhiates, p. 1438
[10] Butler, p. 1074
[11] The NIV Study Bible, p. 1539
[12] Ibid, p. 1538
[13] Goodrick, p. 1544

Chapter 8:

Choose Peace in the Chaos

Day 1: A Path of Peace

Lady BUG trails

Snack to nibble on: John 16:33 (AMP) Be of good cheer [take courage; be confident, certain, undaunted] For I have overcome the world!

I received a very special gift from my very special friend, Sandy, last year. It is a plaque on a tulip stand. The background scene is a beautiful garden with a path leading to a garden gate. I love the quote!

"Wherever life's path leads you, may every step along the way be filled with peace and courage!"

Ahhh...can you imagine how different your life would be if every single step you took was FILLED with peace and courage? How would your daily life change? Do you crave peace? Do you want to be more courageous? If so, begin today's lesson pouring out your heart to God. Tell Him your feelings about these two powerful words — peace and courage. Use the Lady BUG trails margin.

When it comes to peace, let's look to the Prince of Peace for our prime example!

Read John 17. If you have a red-letter edition of the Bible you will notice that the whole chapter is red. This is the longest recorded prayer of Christ. Jesus prayed for Himself in verse 1,

"Father, the time has come!"

What an enormous statement! Jesus had been moving toward this "time" since the day His mother, Mary, tenderly placed Him in the manger. (Well, actually, He'd been preparing for this "time" since before the world began! See John 17:5.)

Throughout John's gospel we see this "time" foreshadowed. Jesus had lived His whole life in preparation for what was about to happen. Read the following passages and write the significance of each.

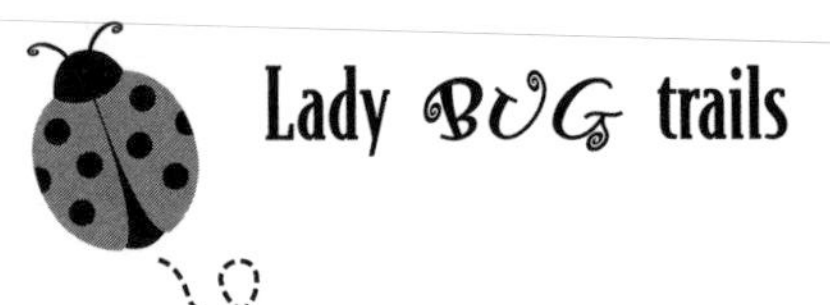

John 2:4 What did Jesus tell His mother, Mary?

John 7:6, 8 What did Jesus tell His brothers?

John 7:25-30 Why did no one lay a hand on Jesus? (v. 30)

John 8:20 Why did no one seize Jesus while He was in the temple area?

John 12:20-36 What would happen to the Son of Man? (vss. 23 and 32)

John 13:1-17 According to verse 1, what did Jesus know? What did He do to show the "full extent of his love" for them?

John 16:25-32 Where did Jesus know He was going? What did He predict His disciples would do?

Now, let's zero in on **John 16:33**. I especially love this verse in the Amplified Version. Notice the phrase "be of good cheer." Cheer in the original Greek language is *tharseo* which means "boldness, courage; be of good cheer, have courage, spoken by way of encouragement." It is equivalent to *tharreo* which means to "be full of hope and confidence!" [1] The NIV usually translates *tharseo* as "take heart" or "take courage."

> *John 16:33 (AMP) I have told you these things, so that in Me you may have [perfect] peace and confidence. In the world you have tribulation and trials and distress and frustration; but be of good cheer [take courage; be confident, certain, undaunted] For I have overcome the world. [I have deprived it of power to harm you and have conquered it for you.]*

What is your favorite part of this passage? Why? Answer in the margin.

I find tremendous comfort knowing:

I have perfect **peace** and confidence IN Jesus!
In this world I will have trouble of all kinds, *BUT*...!
Jesus wants me to take **courage** into my heart!
Jesus has overcome and conquered the world!

What does it mean to have peace and confidence in Jesus?

____

____

"Be of good cheer" means taking courage into your heart. So, how can you actually do this when push comes to shove?

____

____

Jesus said, "I have overcome the world!" Notice that He was claiming His victory before it even happened! He knew after all this time, the "time" had finally come! Jesus knew what was going to happen in the olive grove soon after He finished His prayer. He knew Judas would soon betray Him with a not-so-holy kiss! (Matthew 26:47-49) He also knew He would be arrested and His beloved disciples would turn tail and run! He knew He would soon be hanging on a cruel cross. Yet...He took the time to pray for His disciples.

Read John 17:11 aloud.

Surprisingly, this is the only time the term "Holy Father" is used in the whole Bible. [2] Jesus prays for His disciples' protection! Write verse 11 in your own words.

____

____

____

Jesus also asks God to specifically protect them from whom? (v. 15)

____

I just love verse 17. Fill in the blanks with BIG, BOLD LETTERS!!!

Sanctify them by the ____________!

Your ____________ is ____________!

The Greek word for sanctify is *hagiazo* which has several definitions:

to render or acknowledge, or to be venerable or hallow
to separate from profane things and dedicate to God
consecrate things to God
dedicate people to God
to purify
to cleanse externally
to purify by expiation: free from the guilt of sin
to purify internally by renewing of the soul [3]

In your opinion, which of these definitions best fits the word "sanctify" in John 17:17? Why?

___

___

___

Jesus is essentially asking God to set His disciples apart – to make them holy – by His Word. I think it's hilarious that Jesus is telling God something He already knows full well. **"Your Word is truth!"** Remember, though, this prayer was not one of those while-it-was-still-dark-in-a-solitary-place, one-on-one Father/Son prayers. This prayer was prayed right in front of His disciples. No doubt they were hanging on every Word! Perhaps they needed to hear the truth about Truth! Perhaps we need the same message today!

How does this statement, "Your Word is truth" speak to your heart?

___

___

___

Sir Winston Churchill once said, **"Men occasionally stumble over the truth, but most of them pick themselves up and hurry off as if nothing ever happened!"** [4] What a profound statement! How do we "stumble over" the truth? What are some ways we choose to "hurry off" from the truth? Name some reasons we choose to pretend that we did not encounter the truth.

___

___

When you have free time this week, take a Lady BUG Trail down Truth Thoroughfare! Find as many scriptures as you can to claim for your own. If you stumble over a tasty truthful treat, stop long enough to savor the moment and devour it! Remember Truth is Good Food! Enjoy every bite!

May He fill every Lady BUG step
with His perfect peace and undaunted courage!

Day 2: Living the Lyrics: They'll Know We Are Christians

Yesterday we read John 17. Today we're going to camp out in the last section of this prayer. Read John 17:20. This prayer is also for whom?

___

Shiver me timbers!!! I hope you said your name and mine! This part of the prayer is specifically for us! So, let's tune our ears and pay close attention. **Read John 17:20-23** out loud, if possible. If you highlight in your Bible (it's ok, I promise!) highlight the phrase "may be one" in verses 21 and 22. Now, peek back at John 17:11. Do you see the same phrase? Highlight it, too! Summarize all of those verses into one main idea. Use the Lady BUG trails margin.

When Jesus had an important message to convey He didn't just mention it once and expect His listeners to get it. He usually said it over and over and over again! Turn back a few chapters to John 14. Notice verses 10, 11, and 20. What message does Jesus give His disciples in these verses?

___

___

Sound familiar? Now take a peek at John 10:30. What is the message?

___

Carefully read John 10:31-33. How did the Jews react to this proclamation? What reason did they give Jesus for reacting this way?

___

___

YIKES! Can you imagine having the audacity to tell Jesus (right to His face) "You, ***a mere man***, claim to be God!" and to hurl stones at Him?! The Jews' vehemence was caused by their belief that Jesus was guilty of blasphemy. According to Mosaic Law, what was the punishment for blasphemy? (See Leviticus 24:14-16.)

___

If you're reading from the NIV Bible, circle the very first word of John 10:31. Write it here. _______________ Hmmm...this was not the first time the Jews had picked up stones, literally taking the "law" into their own hands. Place a bookmark in John 10. We'll be right back! Flip a few pages back in history to John 8:58-59. What did Jesus tell the Jews? What was their reaction?

____

____

He's telling us the TRUTH, too, ladies. Allow Jesus to whisper in your ear, "I AM!" He wants you to know and understand this truth. Now, zoom back over to John 10:38. What did Jesus want the Jews to "know" and "understand"?

____

Notice what Jesus says in John 17:23. He wants us to be brought to COMPLETE UNITY! What is the purpose of this complete unity? There are 2 parts. (v. 23)

____

____

Remember, Jesus was praying this prayer for YOU and for ME. Why do you think He used the phrase "complete unity"? In the margin, describe what this means to you.

Go back and skim **John 17** again. Every time you see "world" circle it. How many times does Jesus use the term world? ___________ Great Scot! That's a LOT! Read what Jesus told Nicodemus in **John 3:16-21**. What do these passages say about the world?

____

____

I stand in awe that God loved the world THAT much! Now, He has clearly shown us what He wants us to do. He wants us to be **unified** and show the world God's love! Unity seems to be a HUGE problem in the church today. What's up with that? In your opinion, what are the primary causes? No Rules...Just Write! Use the Lady BUG trails margin.

I've been humming a song all morning as I write this lesson and I just can't hold it in any longer! Let's sing it together. I hope you know it!

They'll Know We Are Christians

(Words and Music by Peter Scholte)

We are one in the Spirit
We are one in the Lord
We are one in the Spirit
We are one in the Lord
And we pray that our unity may one day be restored

Chorus:
And they'll know we are Christians
By our love, by our love
Yes, they'll know we are Christians by our love

We will work with each other
We will work side by side
We will work with each other
We will work side by side
And we'll guard each man's dignity
And save each man's pride

We will walk with each other
We will walk hand in hand
We will walk with each other
We will walk hand in hand
And together we'll spread the news
That God is in our land

Do you believe what you just sang? Before we can "live" the lyrics we must "believe" the lyrics! Read **John 13:34-35**. What part of the song do you think this scripture confirms?

____

____

That is quite a sobering thought! They'll know we are Christians by our love! Yes, they'll know it in our workplace; at the gym; in the grocery store. Yes, they'll know it in the bleachers at the game. They will know it – or NOT – in traffic. They'll know we are Christians by our LOVE! Did this prompt a goose bump? Explain.

____

In my opinion, the most significant line of today's song is the last verse of the first stanza. Fill in the blanks.

And we pray that our __ __ __ __ __ may one day

be __ __ __ __ __ __ __ __ __.

Here is a question to toss around. What is the difference between "creating" unity and "restoring" unity?

____

In Psalm 51:10-12, David pleads with God to "create" in him a pure heart. (This psalm was written after David's rendezvous with Bathsheba. See 2 Samuel 11.) He wants his heart to be made BRAND NEW! David also asks God to "restore" the joy of His salvation. (He admits his sin and pleads for pardon **before** begging for joy. See Psalm 51:1-9.) Perhaps he recalled his harp-playing, sheep-tending days when he knew God was with him, or the day God handed Goliath's head to him! (1 Samuel 17.) He was surely reminiscing about the many victories God had given him! (See 2 Samuel 8:6!)

David is yearning for the joy of his salvation because the memory is beckoning! He said it best himself, "Taste and see that the LORD is good!" (Psalm 34:8) Once you've tasted something THAT good, you have a craving for it forever! This principle is true for us, too. Typically, we yearn for something most when we've delighted in it before! When it's gone we KNOW what we're missing and we ache to have it back! Write your thoughts in the margin.

Let's apply this concept to our song for the day. ***We are one in the Spirit. We are one in the Lord. And, we pray that our unity may one day be***

Lady BUG trails

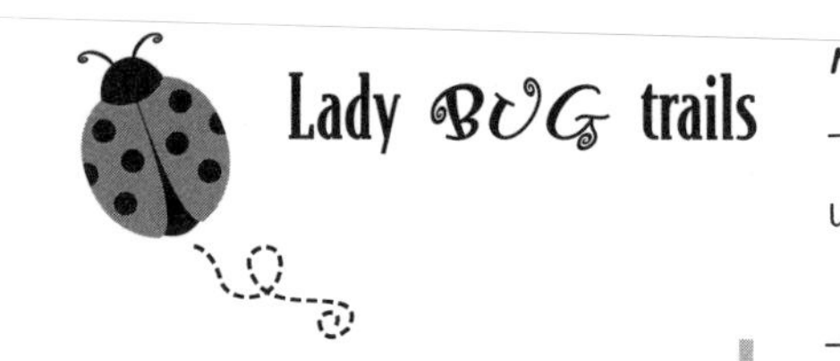

restored! In order to have our unity "restored" we must have a reference point – something to bring back into existence. Have you experienced genuine unity in your church or other group? Do those memories beckon you?

___

___

Unfortunately, many of us haven't seen or experienced enough unity in our own lives to be able to "restore" it to its former condition. We might ask God to CREATE unity rather than restore it! Fortunately, we have details about unity in the early church. I suggest that we pray to God every day for our unity to be "restored" to First Century Christian Unity! My friend and fellow philosopher, Brian Shrock, gave me a springboard of ideas about unity. He believes Christians are to operate as a Unit. (See 1 Corinthians 12:12-31.) If one person wins at the expense of others, all lose! Our Unit shares a common purpose, with our unity being based on LOVE not LEGALISM! Brian gives us a point to ponder, "A restored unity restores people!" Visualize the imagery in this poem.

We are not God's deputies
a pious posse
out to arrest God's people.
We are, instead, God's Medical Team
on a mission
to retrieve the wounded.
United in LOVE,
we humbly approach
The Great Physician.
By His wounds, we are healed!

What is your gut reaction to this poem?

___

___

Several years ago I bought David T. Moore's audio series, "Why Can't You Be Normal...Like ME?" [5] He describes how we attempt to recreate others in our own image, which damages our relationships. He reminds us that most relationships fail miserably when we don't understand and appreciate the uniqueness in others!

Please read Acts 2:42-47 and Acts 4:32-37.

Based on the scriptures in Acts, give an example under each heading of how the First Century Christians displayed unity. Then, give a specific example of how we can "restore" this kind of unity to our families and churches today! There are other scriptures listed for reference. Before you start, chant this phrase, ***"Unity Begins With ME!"***

Unity Does NOT Mean Uniformity! (1 Corinthians 12:12-31)

____

____

Unity Requires Integrity! (1 Chronicles 29:17; Titus 2:6-7)

____

____

Unity Invites Generosity! (2 Corinthians 8:10-15)

____

____

Unity Results in Synergy! (Achieving together what cannot be done individually. Ecclesiastes 4:12)

____

____

Unity Thrives on Humility! (1 Peter 5:5-7)

____

____

Unity Celebrates Diversity! (Romans 12:4-8)

____

____

Unity Demands Sincerity! (Ask Ananias & Sapphira! Acts 5)

____

____

Psalm 133 (NIV)

How good and pleasant it is when brothers live together in unity!
It is like precious oil poured on the head, running down on the beard,
running down on Aaron's beard, down upon the collar of his robes.
It is as if the dew of Hermon were falling on Mount Zion.
For there the LORD bestows his blessing,
even life forevermore.

Day 3: The Light of the World

Snack to nibble on: Matthew 5:14 You are the light of the world!

I love candles. The flickering flame, the warm glow, the pleasant fragrance. I could sit and watch the wick dance for hours. It relaxes me and brings a sense of peace. There's just something about a candle. It helps me "turn down the volume" in my mind. My dear friend Linda Trichter Metcalf, co-author with Tobin Simon of *Writing the Mind Alive* says, "Lighting a candle creates a sacred space...even a single candle will generate a luminous glow that can quiet your mind, focus your attention, and help you turn inward." She teaches writers to "be like the flame and burn with intention!" [6]

Today we're going to be like the flame! We're going to burn with intention as we choose PEACE in the chaos.

If you have a Lady BUG candle, please light it now. If not, any candle will do. (If you're allergic to candles or you just don't like them, be creative! Perhaps a small lamp or flashlight will do the trick!) I wish all of you had a candleholder like mine! My dear friend, Michelle, gave me a precious one last year. It is a Lady BUG candleholder made out of wire mesh with beautiful red wings. I'm staring at her now. She is radiant with light!

Recently, while working on our Bible study about Mary (the Original Lady BUG) it occurred to me that Mary literally carried ***the Light of the world*** around inside of her! Read the following passages and record key words and phrases from each.

John 1:1-9

____

____

____

John 3:19-21

____

____

____

John 8:12

John 9:1-5

John 12:35-36

John 12:46

What can you conclude after reading all of these passages about Jesus?

As you can see, Jesus was the Light of the world! Mary carried Him in her womb for nine months. I would like to suggest that we have a lot more in common with Mary than we may have realized. Let's revisit the precious prayer of Jesus in John 17. Verse 26 is crucial!

Let's not miss a bit of it. We can break the verse down into parts for clearer understanding. Let's personalize and internalize the truth found in this verse.

Jesus continues to make God known to me!
So that the love God has for Jesus may also be in me!
And, that Jesus, Himself, may be in me!

If Jesus, Himself, is IN ME, then, I, like Mary, am carrying the Light of the world around inside of me, too! What a phenomenal thought!

Now, let's take another Lady BUG Trail down Light Lane and see what else the Word has to say about the "light of the world." **Read Matthew 5:14-16**

I feel a song coming on. Are you already singing what I'm singing? **"This Little Light of Mine"!** Surely you know it. If nobody's watching go ahead and do the hand motions. (Or, if somebody's watching maybe they'll join the fun!) Remember what Christ said in Matthew 18:3, "Unless you become like little children you will never enter the kingdom of heaven!" ☺

This little light of mine, I'm gonna let it shine!
This little light of mine, I'm gonna let it shine
This little light of mine, I'm gonna let is shine
Let it shine all the time, let it shine.

Don't let the devil poof it out! I'm gonna let it shine.
Hide it under a bushel, NO! I'm gonna let it shine.

Have you, like me, ever wondered what in the world a "bushel" is? I just had to look it up! Notice these verses from the King James Version of the Bible.

> ***Matthew 5:14-16*** *(KJV) 14 Ye are the light of the world. A city that is set on a hill cannot be hid. 15 Neither do men light a candle, and put it under a* ***bushel****, but on a candlestick; and it giveth light unto all that are in the house. 16 Let your light so shine before men, that they may see your good works, and glorify your Father which is in heaven.*

So, that's where the song writer got the word "bushel." But, what is a bushel? I'm so glad you wanted to know because I'm delighted to tell you! The Greek word for bushel is *modios* which means "a large bowl {sometimes translated basket} that holds about 8 dry quarts." [7]

Let's get back to our passage in Matthew 5:14-16. Notice that Jesus is talking to His disciples. He tells them they are the light of the world. During biblical times people often used small clay lamps that burned olive oil. The oil would be "drawn up" by a wick.

Study this symbolism. What point do you think Jesus was making?

____

____

Let's bring this down a little closer to home. List some reasons why we might hesitate to let our light shine before men.

What does putting our "lamp" on a stand look like in real life? (No right or wrong answers!)

Don your thinking cap and ask yourself this question before writing down your answer. Have you ever hidden your "lamp" under a bowl? If so, why? For how long? What was the end result?

According to verse 16, there are two reasons we let our light shine in the world:

What will the world see?
Who will the world praise?

I'm intrigued that we are told to "let" our light shine rather than "make" our light shine. What, in your opinion, would be the difference?

Day 4: Living the Lyrics: A Simple Prayer

Jesus Christ Himself is light. We, His followers, reflect His light and His glory. **Read Ephesians 5:8-20.** I love verse 19 so much! Let's drink Paul's words and incorporate them into our daily lives. Are you looking for a way to choose peace in the chaos? Here's a wonderful formula!

- **Speak to others with psalms.**
- **Speak to others with hymns.**
- **Speak to others with spiritual songs.**
- **Sing!**
- **Make music in your heart to the Lord!**
- **Always give thanks to God for everything!**
- **Do it all in the name of Jesus, the true Light of the world!**

Speaking of singing, I'm so excited about today's song, "A Simple Prayer." This beautiful song was adapted from the prayer of St. Francis of Assisi. Tune your ears and open the eyes of your heart to hear and see truth!

Prayer of St. Francis

Lord, make me an instrument of your peace,
Where there is hatred, let me sow love;
where there is injury, pardon;
where there is doubt, faith;
where there is despair, hope;
where there is darkness, light;
where there is sadness, joy;
O Divine Master, grant that I may not so much
seek to be consoled as to console;
to be understood as to understand;
to be loved as to love.
For it is in giving that we receive;
it is in pardoning that we are pardoned;
and it is in dying that we are born to eternal life.

What part of this prayer is most difficult to follow in your daily life? Why?

___

___

___

My parents, Paul and Shirley Witt, love to dig in the Word so I solicited their help for the following activity. (My dad preaches for a precious body of believers in Overton, Texas.) The prayer of St. Francis does NOT appear in the Bible but it does contain many biblical truths. We thought it would be quite an expedition to seek and find actual scriptures to match each line of the prayer. Read the passages below. Then, MATCH the main idea from the passage to a line from the prayer. (Write the scripture and its main idea in the blank below each line.) For an extra adrenaline rush, seek and find other scriptures on your own and add them in Lady BUG red!

Seek And Ye Shall Find!

Psalm 30:11	Acts 20:35	1 John 4:11-12
Matthew 13:23	Romans 5:3-5	
Matthew 14:29-31	Romans 6:3-5	
Luke 6:27	Romans 13:12	
Luke 6:37	Romans 14:19	
Luke 23:34	2 Corinthians 1:3-5	

Note: We used the NIV Bible to find these scriptures.

Lord, make me an instrument of your peace.

Where there is hatred, let me sow love.

Where there is injury, pardon (forgiveness).

Where there is doubt, faith.

Where there is despair, hope.

Lady BUG trails

Where there is darkness, light.

Where there is sadness, joy.

Grant that I may not so much seek to be consoled (comforted) as to console (provide comfort).

Grant that I may not so much seek to be understood as to understand.

Grant that I may not so much seek to be loved as to love.

For it is in giving that we receive.

It is in pardoning (forgiving) that we are pardoned (forgiven).

It is in dying that we are born to eternal life.

Now, let's enjoy the lyrics to a beautiful song based on this prayer.

A Simple Prayer

(Adapted from the Prayer of St. Francis of Assisi;
additional words by Robin Lyle)

It is in giving
That we receive
It is in pardoning
That we are pardoned
And it is in dying
That we are born to eternal life

Make me an instrument
Of your peace
I want to know what it's like to follow you
When men look at me
I want them to see
The light of the world inside!

Close your time with the Lord by asking Him to specifically show you how to be an instrument of His peace. Also, reflect upon this question, "When the world looks at me this week, how will I show them the Light of the world inside?"

[1] Zodhiates, pages 718-719
[2] The NIV Study Bible, p. 1630
[3] Thayer and Smith
[4] Churchill
[5] Moore, David T.
[6] Metcalf, p. 29
[7] Goodrick, p. 1572

Chapter 9:

Choose Peace in the Chaos With the Word

Day 1: Peace From the Psalms

Snack to nibble on: Psalm 29:11 The Lord blesses his people with peace!

As we continue down our path of choosing peace in the chaos, let's learn from an expert, the psalmist, shepherd, and king, David! **Read Psalm 4.**

According to verse 8, what will David choose to do even though he is distressed?

____

____

Write verse 8 in Big, Bold letters.

____

____

This would be a great verse to write on one of your Lady BUG Fast Food cards! Display it on your nightstand. Prop it up on your pillow! Tape it to your bathroom mirror. Make a post-it note for the dashboard of your car! What a fantastic example David is for us! David is obviously distressed (v. 1) and is asking for relief. He's frustrated with the "chaos" going on in his life. He realizes that true joy can only be found in the Lord (v.7). He gives it all to God, goes to bed, and rests in PEACE! What a gift David gives to himself, choosing to trust that it is God alone who makes us dwell in safety!

How about you? Have you had a few restless nights lately? Have you been tossing and turning instead of giving it to God? Does David's psalm speak to you? If so, now would be the best time of all to give it to God! Use the margin to pour out your heart.

Let's read another psalm of David. **Psalm 29**. This psalm is more like a hymn of praise! If it's convenient, read this psalm aloud. (For an added bonus, you might even want to stand in His honor while proclaiming this praise!)

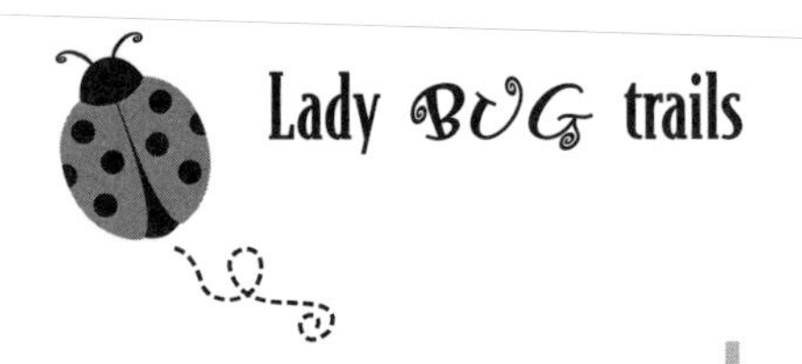

Record your favorite verse of this psalm. Why is it your favorite?

______

______

______

According to verse 11, what does the LORD give to His people?

______

David certainly knew what he was talking about. Read 1 Samuel 30:1-6. Use your magnifying glass to get a closer look at verse 6. What did David find?

______

Ladies, this is gargantuan! David found strength in God! That is exactly where we find our strength, too. It's also extremely important that we remember to share this blessing with our friends and family.

Read 1 Samuel 23:15-16. What did Jonathan help David do?

______

______

Stop and sit back in your chair. Relax and take a few deep breaths. What lesson can you learn from these passages? How can you apply it to your relationships?

______

______

______

I believe the single greatest gift we can give our friends and family is to help them find strength in God! Too often, we are tempted to provide what we think they need instead of letting God do His oh-so-powerful work in their lives! By helping our friend or family member find strength in God we are ultimately seeking peace for them and for ourselves. What a win-win situation!

Now, look back at Psalm 29:11. What does the LORD bless His people with?

______

Ahhh...yes, and what a BLESSING peace is! We all desperately want it. We all desperately NEED it, and yet, how many of us feel like we have it on a regular basis? Reflect upon the deep meaning of this bumper sticker:

No God, No Peace...Know God, Know Peace!

What does it mean to you? Record your thoughts in the Lady BUG trails margin.

Read Psalm 34. Pay special attention to verse 14. David encourages us to:

___ ___ ___ ___ peace!

___ ___ ___ ___ ___ ___ peace!

What are the benefits of seeking and pursuing peace?

Psalm 37:37 ____

Proverbs 12:20 ____

What does Jesus say about "peacemakers" in Matthew 5:9?

____

Write James 3:18. Notice the enormous benefit to "sowing" peace!

____

____

So, we know seeking peace is a great idea. What are ways we can actually put this into practice?

____

____

Read Psalm 37:1-11.

First I must point out my favorite verse in this chapter! It doesn't contain the word peace but it certainly leads to peace! **Write Psalm 37:4.** (This would be another great candidate for your Lady BUG Fast Food cards!)

____

____

Lady BUG Sisters, I have found this scripture to be incredibly and wonderfully true! David was called a "man after God's own heart." He delighted in the Lord regularly! What do you think this passage really means?

____

____

Read **Psalm 37:11.** (This truth is seen again in Matthew 5:5.)

Who will inherit the land and what will they enjoy?

____

The Hebrew word for meek is *anaw*. In this context it means "humble." [1] Here's a question for you. Who was the most humble man on the face of the earth in Numbers 12:3? __________________ What fun to visit our friend, MO, again! After all we studied about him, why do you think he was considered the most humble man on earth?

____

____

Of course, Jesus is the best example of meekness and humility! When you have time this week, take a Lady BUG trail down Meek Lane and see if you can find an example of Jesus being meek or humble! (Hint: The last few verses of Matthew 11 would be a great pit stop!) ☺

Read Psalm 85:8-13. What message do you hear?

____

____

Righteousness and peace kiss each other! Spend some time mulling over this concept.

Now, read Isaiah 32:17. What a beautiful picture! Write your thoughts about this passage. If you're feeling artistic today, you might even want to illustrate this passage in the margin!

Let's close our time together by reading **Psalm 119:161-168.**

Notice verse 165. If I want great peace what do I need to love? What can make me stumble?

____

____

My NIV Study Bible says that great peace **"is complete security and well-being!"** [2] WOW! I want that with my whole heart. Can you think of a time when you felt a sense of complete security and well-being?

____

____

All this talk about choosing peace in the chaos is just that - talk - until you make a choice to make a change in your own life! Pour your heart out to God. Decide on ONE THING you are willing to do this week to choose peace in the chaos. God is ready, willing, and extremely able to bless you with His perfect peace!

____

____

____

____

____

Seek peace and pursue it!

Day 2: Living the Lyrics: Peace Like a River

Our song for today is perky and fun. If you know the hand motions, by all means, you Go Girl with gusto! ☺

As you sing, ask yourself this question after each stanza, **"Do I?"**

Peace Like a River

(author unknown)

I've got peace like a river,
I've got peace like a river,
I've got peace like a river in my soul,
I've got peace like a river,
I've got peace like a river,
I've got peace like a river in my soul.

I've got love like an ocean,
I've got love like an ocean,
I've got love like an ocean in my soul,
I've got love like an ocean,
I've got love like an ocean,
I've got love like an ocean in my soul.

I've got joy like a fountain,
I've got joy like a fountain,
I've got joy like a fountain in my soul,
I've got joy like a fountain,
I've got joy like a fountain,
I've got joy like a fountain in my soul.

I hope you enjoyed the song. Did you give your "little girl within" permission to let it all hang out? Did you remember to ask yourself the question, "Do I?" after each stanza? How do you feel now?

____

____

Here's where I'm going with this activity. I want us to stop and think about what we're singing while we're singing it! Do I have peace like a river in my soul? Do I have love like the ocean? Do I have joy like a fountain? If so, how so? If not, why not? This is a simple song but in order to LIVE THE LYRICS we need to dig a little deeper!

Read Isaiah 66:10-13. Notice God did NOT say He would extend "peace like a puddle" or "peace like a pond." Why do you think He used the imagery "peace like a river"?

____

____

By definition, a river is "a large natural stream of water emptying into an ocean, lake, or other body of water. It is usually fed along its course by converging tributaries. A river can be any stream or abundant flow resembling this, such as *a river of tears*." [3] According to the definition, a river is usually fed by converging tributaries. Converge simply means "to approach the same point from different directions; to tend toward a common conclusion or result." Tributary means "making additions or offering supplies; contributory; subsidiary; a stream or river flowing into a larger stream or river." [4]

Put on your thinking cap. Screw it on real tight! If peace is like a river, what would some "converging tributaries" to that river of peace be?

____

____

Our definition also tells us that a river can be "any stream or abundant flow!" **An abundant flow of peace!** Sounds like heaven on earth to me! Read the following verses aloud. Know in advance these sentiments come straight from my heart to yours! ☺

1 Peter 1:2
Grace and peace be yours in ________________!

Jude 1:2
Mercy, peace, and love be yours in ________________!

How about this love like an ocean business? What does that really mean? Here are a few fun facts to noodle around with. More than 70% of our earth's surface is covered by the ocean! If love is like the ocean, what implications do you see here? Also, the ocean is SALT water. Should our love be "salty" too? There are at least five passages of scripture in the New Testament that mention

Lady BUG trails

the word "salt." Take a Lady BUG trail in the margin! Saunter down Salt Street and savor some seasoned sustenance from Scripture! (Hint: The food for thought is waiting for you in Matthew, Mark, Luke, Colossians, and James!)

Finally, let's spend a few moments on this **Joy = Fountain** idea. When you sing, "I've got joy like a fountain" what kind of fountain comes to mind? Is it a water fountain spraying beautiful streams of refreshing water high into the air? Or, is it more like a drinking fountain providing a steady stream of thirst-quenching "living water" just when you need it most? Perhaps your joy is more like a soda fountain! Sadly, you may be realizing your "fountain" is all dried up! Whatever the case, consider your joy and compare it to the fountain of your choice.

___

___

___

I wish I could read each and every response. Lean in and I'll tell you my delicious little secret. When I sing, "I've got joy like a fountain" I picture a **chocolate fountain**! (Friends and family reading this, I bet you're not surprised! ☺) Chocolate and I go waaaaaaaaaaaay back!

Recently, our family attended a wedding. At the reception we were pleasantly surprised to find an assortment of fruit along with marshmallows, pretzels, and delectable cream puffs. These were beautifully arranged next to a basket of long bamboo skewers. At the center of attention stood a glorious Chocolate Fountain! It resembled a 3-tiered wedding cake with molten chocolate cascading off of each tier. We stood in line watching the guests dip their skewered fruit and other goodies into the chocolate flow. Licking our lips, my children and I patiently waited our turn! It was, indeed, worth the wait! We skewered and dipped (and dripped) to our heart's content, becoming fast friends with the Flowing Fondue!

Here is a thought to simmer on the back burner. Aunt Phyllis shared with me a SECRET about the Chocolate Fountain. If you want ordinary chocolate to flow smoothly and consistently over the fountain tiers, you need to add some **OIL** to your chocolate! Woo Woo! What a life application this is for me! How could you apply this imagery?

___

___

Read Psalm 45:7. This verse is smack dab in the middle of a wedding song! (I bet they would have enjoyed a Fondue Fountain, too!) God anointed the king with a special kind of oil. This oil was more delightful than the aromatic oils used to anoint his head and body on his wedding day. [5] Specifically, what kind of oil did God use?

____

What did the shepherd-psalmist David so eloquently say about oil in the best-loved psalm of all time? (Psalm 23:5) What does this mean to you?

____

____

____

Phillip Keller, in his fabulous book, *A Shepherd Looks at Psalm 23*, describes in vivid detail how he cared for his sheep. During the summer, hordes of insects would attack his sheep. For relief from this agony, the sheep would beat their heads against trees and thrash around against anything to alleviate their misery. Without the shepherd's intervention the sheep would live in torment! Shepherd Keller "anointed" his sheep with OIL mixed with sulfur and tar. He recalled, "What an incredible transformation this would make among the sheep! Once the oil had been applied to the sheep's head there was an immediate change in behavior!" He stresses that this was not just a one-time application. It had to be repeated frequently. He likens this "oil" to God's gracious Holy Spirit saying, "It is this daily anointing of God's gracious Spirit upon my mind which produces in my life such personality traits as joy, contentment, love, patience, gentleness and peace." [6]

Galatians 5:22 lists the fruit of the Spirit. What are the first three in the list? Write them in the margin or highlight them in your Bible. Shazam! There are the three special words from our song of the day! It's important to remember that this fruit is produced by the Holy Spirit. Why is it crucial for us to have a "daily" anointing of the Holy Spirit?

____

____

Our shepherd friend Phillip Keller also describes a time when his flock became infected with a highly contagious disease. This time each animal had to be "completely submerged" in the OIL antidote. The loving shepherd bought a "huge dipping tank" and proceeded to dip each and every sheep, making sure their heads were "plunged under completely." [7]

Eureka! Talk about oil of joy! Imagine those sheep singing, "I've Got JOY Like a Chocolate Fountain" as they were emerging from the dip! ☺ Write 1 Peter 1:8-9 (NIV).

____

____

____

____

____

John Gill believes this inexpressible and glorious joy is the kind of joy that is "better experienced than expressed." It's a joy that strangers know nothing of, but is such that Christians themselves can't convey proper ideas of it to others. This joy in BELIEVING in Him passes all understanding. The joy of the hypocrites lasts only a moment, but genuine, Christian joy is always abiding! It is by this inexpressible and glorious joy Christians may catch a glimpse of what heaven itself will be! [8]

Close your time in prayer. Soul search with The Good Shepherd. Explore with Him the answers to these questions. Is my peace like a river or a pond? Is my love like the ocean or a puddle? Is my joy like a fountain or a desert? Then ask Him to anoint you (a "double dip" if you dare!) with His soul-reviving oil of JOY!

____

____

____

____

____

____

____

____

Day 3: Peas in My River

Snack to nibble on: Isaiah 66:12 "I will extend peace to her like a river!"

It happened on a Wednesday night sometime last year. I was teaching a three-year-old class, standing in the middle of the room, surrounded by sixteen tots, singing "I've Got Peace Like a River" with hand motions in mid-air. All of a sudden the memory hit me like a bolt of lightning! I could picture my own daughter, Alli, years earlier singing this same song in her high chair. Her version was slightly different, though. She was singing, "I've Got Peas in My River...." I can still picture her precious face. I can still hear her tender toddler voice. I can still feel the giggles we shared about a river of peas.

Here's a question for you. Do you ever feel like you have "peas in your river" instead of "peace like a river"?

❑yes ❑no ❑no clue what you're talking about

I'm guessing there's not much "peace" in a river filled with peas! What does this river look like? How does it smell? What is the texture of the water? Now, dip your toe into the river. Would you like to take a swim? Jot down your first thoughts. No Rules...Just write!

What fun it would be to read ALL of your descriptions! Likely, no two rivers would be exactly alike! Undoubtedly, peas in a river would turn the water an ugly green color (unless yours was filled with black-eyed peas!) ☺ Was your river mushy, gushy, soupy, or goopy?

Have you ever heard the term "mondegreen" before? According to Wikipedia, a **mondegreen** is the mishearing (usually accidental) of a phrase, such that it acquires a new meaning. The word mondegreen is itself a mondegreen. As a child, the writer Sylvia Wright heard a Scottish ballad titled "The Bonny Earl of Murray." One stanza, she believed, went like this:

Ye Highlands and Ye Lowlands/ Oh Where hae you been?/ They hae slay the Earl of Murray/ And Lady Mondegreen.

She thought it was romantic and poetic that Lady Mondegreen had perished with her lord in medieval Scotland. Years later she learned the "correct" lyrics for the song realizing they had actually slain the Earl of Murray and ***"laid him on the green."*** Sylvia Wright collected similar mishearings of song lyrics and published an article about them in 1954, coining the word "mondegreen." [9]

Why all this talk about mondegreens in a Bible study? I want us to become more aware of what we're singing and why we're singing it! Do you recognize any of these phrases from beloved hymns? If so, fill in the original lyrics. Feel free to add a few of your own in the extra space provided.

Mondegreen	Original Lyrics
I've Got Peas in My River	I've Got Peace Like a River
Low in the "gravy" lay	
Bringing in the "Sheets"	
Gladly The Cross-Eyed Bear	
There Is A "Bomb" in Gilead	
Now let us...have a little "chocolate" Jesus!	
It Is Swell With My Soul	

I hope you had a chuckle or two. My mother said it was quite hilarious to hear my brother ask, "Why should we come rejoicing, bringing in the sheets?" (From the hymn "Bringing in the Sheaves.") Do you have a story to share?

____

____

____

Imagine 8-year-old Johnny sitting on his church pew trying his best to reconcile how a "bomb" in Gilead can make the wounded HOLE! (From the hymn "There Is a Balm in Gilead.")

Here's my point. It's funny when children get confused and sing the wrong words. But, sometimes, even as adults, we sing, sing, sing and we have no idea what we're singing!

Yesterday we discussed how to live the lyrics of that great song, "Peace Like a River." Today we're going to explore this idea further.

Read Isaiah 48:17-19 (NIV).

What does God teach us? (v. 17) ______________________

Where does God direct us? (v. 17) ______________________

Analyze verse 18 carefully.

"If only you had paid _ _ _ _ _ _ _ _ _ to my

_ _ _ _ _ _ _ _, your _ _ _ _ _ would have been like

a _ _ _ _ _, your _ _ _ _ _ _ _ _ _ _ _ _ _

like the _ _ _ _ _ of the sea!

The Israelites could have had peace like a river if they had made a different choice. What was their choice? How can we apply this truth to our lives today?

____

____

____

Lady BUG trails

Read Isaiah 66:12-13.

Many scholars believe this prophecy is for the church. Summarize these verses in your own words.

___

___

___

___

Read 2 Corinthians 1:3-7. What do these passages say about God? Why does He comfort us? How does our comfort overflow to others?

___

___

___

The God of all comfort comforts us **so that** we can comfort others! Through Christ our comfort overflows! Hmmm...could this be peace like a river overflowing?!! Share your thoughts.

___

___

___

___

___

___

This week, take a few minutes to ponder. Is your "river" filled with PEACE or PEAS? Perhaps it's time to have a little "chocolate" Jesus and declare once and for all, "It is Swell With My Soul!" ☺

Day 4: Living the Lyrics: There is a Balm in Gilead

Lady BUG trails

Read Jeremiah 33:1-9 (NIV).

Take a close look at the second half of verse 6. God makes two promises. What are they?

I will _______________ my people.

I will let them enjoy _______________ ____________ and security.

John Gill interprets Jeremiah 33:6 in the following way:

Verse 6 refers to the church of God, the members of it, typified by Jerusalem; and it is to be understood of the healing of their spiritual maladies, the diseases of sin, through the blood of the Messiah, who should arise with healing in his wings; that is, with remission of sin, which is often meant by healing in Scripture: Christ is the physician; his blood the balm in Gilead, which being applied to those that are diseased with sin, to sin sick souls, it makes an effectual cure of them; so that they shall not say they are sick, because their iniquities are forgiven them! [10]

Woo Hoo! Today we will rejoice about the balm (not bomb) in Gilead! Are you familiar with the song? Sing the song if you know the tune or speak the lyrics aloud as beautiful prose.

There Is a Balm in Gilead

(Traditional Spiritual)

There is a balm in Gilead to make the wounded whole
There is a balm in Gilead to heal the sin-sick soul

Sometimes I feel discouraged, and think my work's in vain
But, then the Holy Spirit revives my soul again.

If you cannot preach like Peter, if you cannot pray like Paul
You can tell the love of Jesus and say, "He died for all."

What is your favorite verse and why?

____

____

____

____

____

____

Balm was a substance known in the ancient world for its aromatic and medicinal properties. Some say it was a "soothing ointment" used for healing wounds. Gilead means "rugged" country. It was especially famous for its "balm of Gilead" likely derived from the resin of a small balsam tree. [11]

Read Jeremiah 8:18-22.

Poor Jeremiah! I feel his pain. I hear his heartache. He is crushed because his people are crushed (v. 21). Now, let's fast forward and read Jeremiah 30:17. What does the LORD promise to do?

____

____

We know that God forgives our sins and heals our diseases. This very fact can fill our hearts with peace! Read David's beautiful words in **Psalm 103**. Write your favorite verses on the lines below!

____

____

____

____

____

____

____

____

Oh, my soul is praising the Lord! I never want to forget all His benefits! He forgives me and heals me and redeems my life from the hideous pit! He crowns me with love! He crowns me with compassion! He fills me to the brim with HIM! His love is ALWAYS with me! His righteousness is with my children!

Ask yourself this question and take your time with the answer. Why do we have such a hard time choosing PEACE in the midst of all these glorious benefits???????

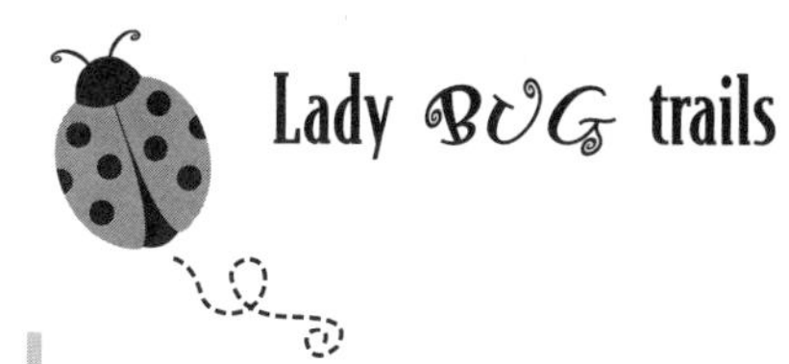

According to Jeremiah 33:9, what will God provide? How will the people react?

I stand in awe at the abundant prosperity and PEACE that is ours to enjoy. Jesus Christ is our Great Physician. (Mark 2:17) By His wounds we are healed!

Write Isaiah 53:5.

His blood is the "balm" that will heal our sin-sick souls if only we will bring the wound to Him and not hide it! Close today's lesson asking the Great Physician for some soothing salve for your soul.

Lady BUG trails

---

[1] Baker, p. 852

[2] The NIV Study Bible, p. 921

[3] Morris

[4] Ibid

[5] The NIV Study Bible, p. 831

[6] Ibid

[7] Ibid

[8] Gill, 1 Peter 1:8

[9] Mondegreen

[10] Gill, Jeremiah 33:6

[11] Butler

Chapter 10:

Choose Peace in the Chaos With Prayer

Day 1: A Choice to Rejoice

Snack to nibble on: Philippians 4:7 And the peace of God, which transcends all understanding, will guard your hearts and your minds in Christ Jesus!

Read Philippians 4:1-9.

We will camp out in these passages this week and look at each verse individually. It intrigues me that the apostle Paul wrote this letter to the Philippians while he was in prison!

Read Philippians 1:12-14.

If anyone knew how to choose peace in the chaos, it would have certainly been the apostle Paul! According to him, what impact did his imprisonment have on the gospel? (v. 12)

____

____

____

Who was Paul in chains for? (v. 13) ______________________

Encouraged by Paul's example, how did the Christians speak the Word of God? (v. 14)

____

Study Philippians 4:4 carefully. Notice that Paul reminds us to rejoice, not once, but twice! Apparently, the message bears repeating!

Rejoice in the Lord always.
I will say it again: Rejoice!

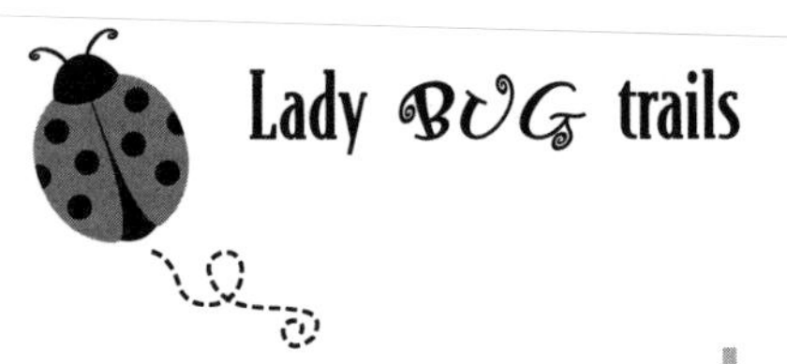

If you know the song "Rejoice in the Lord Always," now would be a great time to break out in song! Feel free to hum it the rest of the day! ☺

Read Habakkuk's Prayer. (Habakkuk 3:1-19)

Summarize Habakkuk's prayer in your own words (paying particular attention to verses 17-19). If you want to, write your own modern day prayer using a similar format. No Rules...Just Write! in the margin.

According to James 1:2-4; 12 what possible reasons could we have for "rejoicing in the Lord" even during difficult times?

____

____

____

____

Now, read 1 Peter 4:12-19. According to verse 13, why should we rejoice when we participate in the sufferings of Christ?

____

____

____

What does verse 14 say?

____

____

Frankly, it's hard for us to have a clue what true suffering was like for the early Christians. Let's consider how these scriptures apply to us today! Have you been "insulted" because of the name of Christ recently? Have you suffered because you're a Christian? If so, how?

____

____

____

____

Let's hold on to the promise that the Spirit of glory and of God rests on us! Now, let's look at Philippians 4:5.

Let your gentleness be evident to all.

It has been said that gentleness is "Christ-like consideration for others."[1] We know that Christ demonstrated His meekness (humility) throughout scripture. We also know that He was gentle. What does Paul say about Jesus in 2 Corinthians 10:1?

What does Jesus say about Himself in Matthew 11:29?

So what does "done right" look like? In other words, how can we let our gentleness be evident to all? Name some outward expressions of gentleness.

Write Proverbs 15:1. Allow this principle to percolate for a bit. Have you witnessed this truth in action recently?

It is extremely important for church leaders to be gentle and considerate. (See 1 Timothy 3:3; Titus 3:2) Why do you think this is true?

Read Ephesians 4:1-6. Name some ways we can be "completely humble and gentle" in our daily Christian walk.

Read Colossians 3:12-17. WOW! This passage is packed FULL of goodies for us to remember. Notice verse 12 says for us to "clothe" ourselves with gentleness. Imagine what a Gentleness Garment would look like and feel like! Describe it here, and if you're feeling artistic today, draw your design in the margin!

Notice Colossians 3:15. Let the "**peace of Christ"** rule in your hearts! This is the only place in the entire Bible where the phrase "peace of Christ" is used. Take a moment to ponder the peace of Christ. How do we let His peace rule in our hearts?

____

____

____

____

____

____

Read Ephesians 2:11-22. Now, use your magnifying glass to examine verse 14 very closely. Fill in the TRUTH below!

______________________________ IS our peace!

Read John 14:15-31.

Now, let's read John 14:27 from the Amplified Bible:

> *Peace I leave with you; My [own] peace I now give and bequeath to you. Not as the world gives do I give to you. Do not let your hearts be troubled, neither let them be afraid. [Stop allowing yourselves to be agitated and disturbed; and do not permit yourselves to be fearful and intimidated and cowardly and unsettled!] John 14:27 (AMP)*

Let's take these words to heart. Jesus wants us to **stop** allowing ourselves to be agitated and disturbed. Ask yourself these questions. What am I agitated about? What disturbs me most? Am I feeling fearful, intimidated, cowardly, or unsettled today? Choose ONE of these words and pray to the Prince of Peace about it. Remember, He wants us to choose peace! Ask Him to show you how!

____

____

____

____

Day 2: A Society of Anxiety

Snack to nibble on: Philippians 4:5 Let your gentleness be evident to all. The Lord is near.

The last part of verse 5 is crucial!

The Lord is near.

Stop and ask yourself this question, "Do I believe it?" Do I really and truly believe the Lord is near? If so, am I LIVING like I believe it?

Read the following passages recording each truth that you find. Consider how this truth applies to your unique situation.

Psalm 119:151

Psalm 145:18

James 4:8

I love knowing that God is near to ALL who call on Him in truth! What comfort do you find in these scriptures?

Let's move to the heart of the matter. ANXIETY! I believe we live in a society of anxiety! Read Philippians 4:6.

Do not be anxious about anything!

Hmmm...look at that word anything. What would that encompass?

Do we take this passage seriously? Make a Lady BUG Fast Food card out of Philippians 4:6. Devour it. Let it nourish your mind, body, and soul! What is your heart's response to this verse?

Read Ecclesiastes 11:10 (NIV). What shall we do with anxiety?

I absolutely adore the word BANISH! I hope you have access to a NIV Bible for this verse. Some of the other translations use a weenie word like "remove" instead of banish in this context. I don't know about you, but when I "remove" my anxiety it usually finds a way to move right back in! Banish is also more meaningful to me than the phrase "put away." When I put away my anxiety, unfortunately I know right where it is and sometimes I'm tempted to retrieve it!

Banish, by definition, means "to force to leave...by official decree; exile; to drive away; expel!" [2] Big, bad, bold **BANISH** means forced departure! (Polite phraseology like, "Would you care to leave now, Anxiety?" simply will not do!) Usually, banish means exiling something or someone to someplace far, far away! Also, permission must be granted for the banished one to return! Considering these definitions for banish, what are three specific ways you can banish anxiety from your heart?

David had a great solution for banishing anxiety. **Read Psalm 139:23-24.**

David realized that God knew him better than he even knew himself. Notice that he asked God for specific actions!

Search me!
Know my heart!
Test me!
Know my anxious thoughts!
See if there is any offensive way in me!
Lead me in the way everlasting!

I wonder what would happen if we woke up every morning with this prayer on our tongue! How do you think life would be different?

Now, read **Psalm 94:18-19.** Re-write this verse in your own words. Do you remember a specific instance when this verse was true for you? Recall the details. Give Him the glory!

____

____

____

____

____

____

____

____

According to Proverbs 12:25, what does an anxious heart do? What combats the anxiety? Have you seen this truth in your life?

____

____

____

____

Write 1 Peter 5:6-7.

____

____

____

____

____

____

God **CARES!** Never doubt that fact for a moment. Why can we cast our cares on Him? Because He cares for us! Do you have a few "cares" that need "casting" today? God's ready to listen. CAST AWAY!

____

____

____

____

____

Day 3: Living the Lyrics: Peace, Perfect Peace

Many moons ago in 1875, Edward Henry Bickersteth heard a sermon while vacationing in Harrogate, England. The minister, Canon Gibbon, taught from Isaiah 26:3 presumably from the King James Bible.

> Isaiah 26:3 (KJV) Thou wilt keep him in perfect peace, whose mind is stayed on thee: because he trusteth in thee.

The minister piqued Edward Bickersteth's interest by explaining that "perfect peace" in the original Hebrew was, in fact, the same word used twice, (salom, salom) indicating absolute perfection! (In today's language we might say Peace Squared!)

This intriguing idea was still on Edward's mind later that same day as he visited a dying relative. In an effort to provide comfort, Edward read Isaiah 26:3 to the dying man, then sat down by his bedside and composed the lyrics to our present-day hymn, "Peace, Perfect Peace." Edward Bickersteth read these lyrics – in question form, just as they appear today – to the man. Perhaps these were the last words he heard before Jesus called him "to Heaven's perfect peace!." [3]

There is an ancient Chinese proverb that gives me great cause for pause. "One who asks a question is a fool for five minutes; one who does not ask a question remains a fool forever!" What is your gut reaction to this proverb?

____

____

____

____

____

Sing "Peace, Perfect Peace." If you are familiar with this song, ask God to give you temporary amnesia so you can read these words for the very first time. Meditate on the lyrics. Ask yourself the questions! See if you agree with Albert Edward Bailey who said, "The questions form a series of challenges to our faith. In each case Jesus is the key that resolves the dilemma!" [4]

Peace, Perfect Peace

(Words: Edward H. Bickersteth; Music: George T. Caldbeck)

Peace, perfect peace, in this dark world of sin?
The blood of Jesus whispers peace within.

Peace, perfect peace, by thronging duties pressed?
To do the will of Jesus, this is rest.

Peace, perfect peace, with sorrows surging round?
On Jesus' bosom naught but calm is found.

Peace, perfect peace, with loved ones far away?
In Jesus' keeping we are safe, and they.

Peace, perfect peace, our future all unknown?
Jesus we know, and He is on the throne.

Peace, perfect peace, death shadowing us and ours?
Jesus has vanquished death and all its powers.

It is enough: earth's struggles soon shall cease,
And Jesus call us to Heaven's perfect peace.

In order to help us LIVE THE LYRICS of this great song we are going to re-write this song using our own personal, modern-day language. The activity is simple. The results may be PROFOUND! Take your time. Write your "new song" in the space provided. You may want to have a dictionary and thesaurus handy to decipher some of the archaic language. Keep a concordance nearby in case you want to look up some scriptures that undoubtedly will pop into your mind!

Now hear this! Your song does not have to rhyme! It does not have to be perfect (like His peace!). ☺ This is just a way to internalize the message. Please write your name in the blank provided to claim OWNERSHIP of your new song. As the saying goes, we are what we eat. I would like to suggest that we are also what we sing! Music feeds the soul. Write ON!

______________'s Version of "Peace, Perfect Peace"

Stanza 1:

Peace, perfect peace, in this dark world of sin?
The blood of Jesus whispers peace within.

Your version:

____

____

Stanza 2:

Peace, perfect peace, by thronging duties pressed?
To do the will of Jesus, this is rest.

Your version:

____

____

Stanza 3:

Peace, perfect peace, with sorrows surging round?
On Jesus' bosom naught but calm is found.

Your version:

____

____

Stanza 4:

Peace, perfect peace, with loved ones far away?
In Jesus' keeping we are safe, and they.

Your version:

____

____

Stanza 5:

Peace, perfect peace, our future all unknown?
Jesus we know, and He is on the throne.

Your version:

____

____

Stanza 6:

Peace, perfect peace, death shadowing us and ours?
Jesus has vanquished death and all its powers.

Your version:

____

____

Stanza 7:

It is enough: earth's struggles soon shall cease,
And Jesus call us to Heaven's perfect peace.

Your version:

____

____

Write Psalm 40:3 in the margin. (And, while you're at it, thank God for putting a new song in your mouth!)

I would LOVE to see your song! (If you have my e-mail address, please send it to me!) How did you like that activity? Did you hate it a lot? Or, did you love straining your brain? Maybe you skipped it altogether. (No worries. God still loves you!) Did you find the challenge refreshing? Or, did it feel ho-hum? Did you have a hard time understanding Bickersteth's message? Or, did his lyrics prick your heart?

____

____

____

That phrase "thronging duties pressed" is a curious one! To shed a little light on the subject, let's dust off our King James Bibles and take a peek at this word in context.

> Mark 3:9 (KJV) And he spake to his disciples, that a small ship should wait on him because of the multitude, lest they should **throng** him.

> Luke 8:45 (KJV) And Jesus said, "Who touched me?" When all denied, Peter and they that were with him said, "Master, the multitude **throng** thee and press thee, and sayest thou, Who touched me?"

For more clarity, look at those passages in your favorite version. Based on this context what do you think throng means? In the margin, name some of the "thronging duties" pressing on you.

Read Matthew 11:28-30. What is Christ's yoke? What about this yoke is easy? Why, in your opinion, does He say His burden is light?

____

____

Holman describes a yoke as "a wooden frame placed on the backs of animals to make them pull in tandem." [5] In Biblical times, an inexperienced ox was often "yoked" with a well-trained, more experienced ox. (I picture this like a mentor/mentee program!) The mentor ox did all the real pulling and plowing while the mentee ox plowed alongside. As Christian sisters we are "yoked" together with the best Mentor Ox of them all! He does the plowing and we live and learn alongside of Him. It's only when we choose to tug in the opposite direction that the "yoke" becomes less than comfy. [6] In fact, that's always where the rub comes in! Amen?!

Unlike the Pharisees, Jesus did not heap a heavy load of legalistic luggage on the backs of His followers. (See Matthew 12:1-14.) On the contrary, what He asks us to "shoulder" is light. Jesus wants more than anything for us to come to Him for rest! He wants us to wrap His yoke around our weary shoulders and learn from Him! Notice this is a CHOICE. He tells us to "take His yoke upon us" which requires initiation on our part. Jesus demonstrates gentleness and humility. It's our task to take the yoke and learn the lessons. Then, we will "find" much-needed rest for our souls!

Read Matthew 8:24. What was Jesus doing while the disciples were freaking out about the furious storm wreaking havoc on their boat? What does this tell you about Jesus? Do you crave that kind of calm like I do?

____

____

____

____

Jesus Christ certainly knows how to choose peace in the chaos! Close your time in prayer. Remember to thank your Mighty Mentor for His Perfect Peace.

Here's a gift of poetry from my heart to yours! Thank you for joining me on this journey. I appreciate you!

Thronging burdens pressing?
Gloomy? Weary? Scared?
Take His yoke – it's easy
Choose Peace Squared!

Day 4: Transcending Understanding

Snack to nibble on: Philippians 4:6 Do not be anxious about anything, but in everything, by prayer and petition, with thanksgiving, present your requests to God.

Let's dive into the last part of verse 6.

But, in everything by prayer and petition, WITH THANKSGIVING, present your requests to God.

The Greek word for petition is *deesis,* meaning "to make known one's particular need; to pray for particular benefits." [7] Pray and petition with thanksgiving! What does this look like? Sound like? Feel like? Use the margin to record your thoughts.

Remember Colossians 3:15? Let the peace of Christ rule in your hearts! What are the last three words of that verse?

__________ ________ ____________________________!

I love Colossians 3:17. Most of us probably have it memorized. "Whatever we do in word or deed, do it all in the name of the Lord." But, let's not forget the rest of that verse! What does the last part of verse 17 tell us to do?

____

Giving thanks is HUGE! **1 Thessalonians 5:16-18** tells us to be joyful always, pray continually, and give thanks in ALL circumstances! Why do we do this? Read the last part of verse 18 for the answer!

____

Let's head back to our camp in Philippians 4. I think we could spend a whole week on verse 7 alone!

And the peace of God, which transcends all understanding, will guard your hearts and your minds in Christ Jesus!

Remember Isaiah 26:3 from day 3? Let's take a look at this same verse in the Amplified Bible.

You will guard him and keep him in perfect and constant peace whose mind [both its inclination and its character] is stayed on You, because he commits himself to You, leans on You, and hopes confidently in You. Isaiah 26:3 (AMP)

Take your time and savor the FOOD in this passage. In your own words, what is the main message?

____

____

____

I want God to guard me and keep me in perfect and constant peace. How about you? CONSTANT peace! Wouldn't that be grand? When do you crave peace most?

____

____

Isaiah 26:3 gives us three ways (my daughter would say these are three DOING WORDS!) to keep our minds focused on God. In order to have perfect and constant peace with God we need to:

Commit ______________________.

Lean ______________________.

Hope ______________________.

<u>COMMIT.</u> What is a commitment? What is another word for commitment?

____

____

Over the years you have undoubtedly made many commitments. Pick only ONE. Closely examine the nuts and bolts of that commitment. What did it take to stick to your commitment? What were your struggles? Successes? What lessons have you learned about commitment? Can you apply those to your relationship with God? Answer these questions in the margin.

<u>LEAN!</u> How do we "lean" on God? What is the difference between making a commitment to God and leaning on Him?

____

____

Write Proverbs 3:5.

HOPE CONFIDENTLY. This is a biggie! How can we "hope confidently" in God? What is the difference between "hope" and "confident hope"?

Write Psalm 71:5.

Read Hebrews 4:16. How do we approach the throne of grace? What will we receive in our time of need? Does this speak to your heart?

Notice Philippians 4:7 says that the peace of God "transcends all understanding." Have you ever had a feeling of "peace" that you couldn't quite describe? You couldn't quite wrap your mind around it? That, sisters, is the Peace of GOD! We are not supposed to understand it! If you've experienced that peace, describe the circumstances in the margin.

Let's take a closer look at Paul's encouraging words in Philippians 4:8. These are the things Paul encourages us to think about. Someone I know actually put this scripture on their television set! Can you imagine how many times they switched the channels or just ended up turning the tube OFF? Let's personalize this scripture. Next to each phrase list two things that fit that category. (i.e., list two true things, two noble things, etc.) This may take a little brain jogging. GREAT! Jogging is good for the soul!

Whatever is TRUE!

Whatever is NOBLE!

Whatever is RIGHT!

Whatever is PURE!

Whatever is LOVELY!

Whatever is ADMIRABLE!

If anything is EXCELLENT or PRAISEWORTHY!

Paul really puts himself on the line with verse 9. He encourages his readers to emulate his behavior! How many of us could be so bold?

And the God of peace will be with you.

Notice the phrase change. In verse 7 the "peace of God" will guard our hearts and minds. In verse 9 the "God of peace" will be with us! Write **1 Thessalonians 5:23-24** in the margin. (Notice the confidence Paul has in God!)

Take a few moments to look back over your notes from the lessons this week. What changes will you make in your daily life that will enable you to choose PEACE in the chaos? Praise God in advance for the choices He will help you make!

May the God of peace be with you all!

---

[1] The NIV Study Bible, p. 1808
[2] Morris
[3] Peace, Perfect Peace
[4] Bailey
[5] Butler
[6] Hindson, p. 1279
[7] Zodhiates, p. 399

Chapter 11:

Day 1: Living the Lyrics - I Come to the Garden Alone

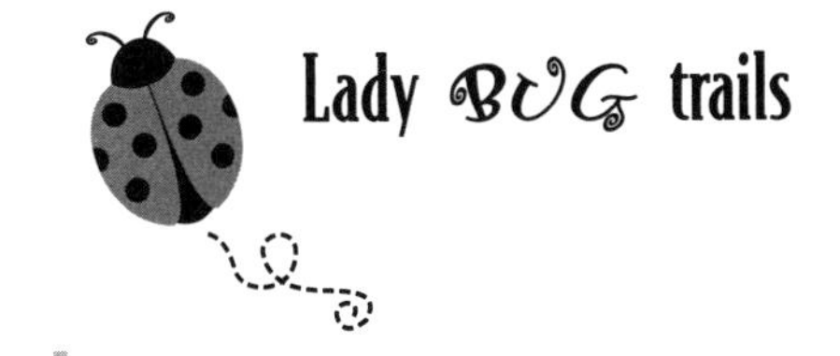

Welcome to the garden! I'm so glad you came! Our song of the day is one of the best-loved hymns ever written. Sing the song. Savor every sentiment. Linger over the lyrics. Make melody in your heart or sing aloud with your best vibrato!

I Come to the Garden Alone

(Formerly "In the Garden" by C. Austin Miles, 1912)

I come to the garden alone,
While the dew is still on the roses;
And the voice I hear, falling on my ear,
The Son of God discloses.

And He walks with me, and He talks with me,
And He tells me I am His own;
And the joy we share as we tarry there,
None other has ever known.

He speaks, and the sound of His voice
Is so sweet the birds hush their singing;
And the melody that He gave to me,
Within my heart is ringing.

I'd stay in the garden with Him,
Tho the night around me be falling,
But He bids me go; Thru the voice of woe
His voice to me is calling.

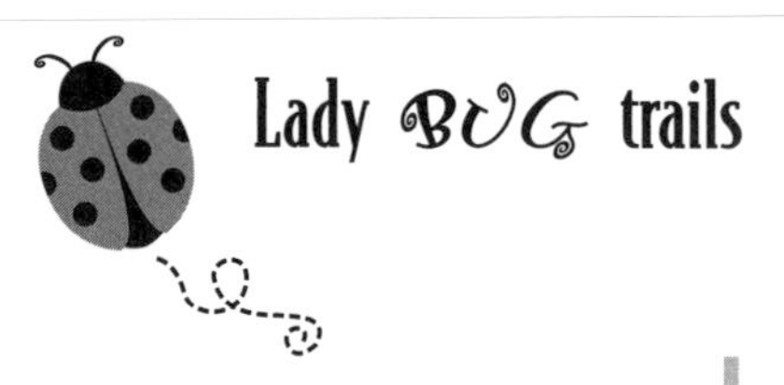

I have known our song of the day for many years but did not know the full story behind it until recently. The story is fascinating!

The original title for this song was **"In The Garden."** It was written by Charles Austin Miles in 1912 in response to a request by his publisher, Adam Geibel, to write a hymn text that would be "sympathetic in tone, breathing tenderness in every line; one that would bring hope to the hopeless, rest for the weary, and downy pillows to dying beds!" [1]

Hmmm...how could a song bring "downy pillows" to dying beds? No Rules...Just Write!

____

____

____

____

____

____

When asked what inspired him to write this song, Charles Austin Miles gave the following testimony:

"One day in April, 1912, I was seated in the dark room, where I kept my photographic equipment and organ. I drew my Bible toward me; it opened at my favorite chapter, John 20—whether by chance or inspiration let each reader decide. That meeting of Jesus and Mary {Magdalene} had lost none of its power and charm. As I read it that day, I seemed to be part of the scene. I became a silent witness to that dramatic moment in Mary's life, when she knelt before her Lord, and cried, Rabboni!

My hands were resting on the Bible while I stared at the light blue wall. As the light faded, I seemed to be standing at the entrance of a garden, looking down a gently winding path, shaded by olive branches. A woman in white, with head bowed, hand clasping her throat, as if to choke back her sobs, walked slowly into the shadows. It was Mary! As she came to the tomb, upon which she placed her hand, she bent over to look in, and hurried away.

John, in flowing robe, appeared, looking at the tomb; then came Peter, who entered the tomb, followed slowly by John. As they departed, Mary reappeared; leaning her head upon her arm at the tomb, she wept. Turning herself, she saw Jesus standing; so did I! I knew it was He. She knelt before Him, with arms outstretched and looking into His face cried, Rabboni!

I awakened in sunlight, gripping the Bible, with muscles tense and nerves vibrating. Under the inspiration of this vision I wrote as quickly as the words could be formed the poem exactly as it has since appeared. That same evening I wrote the music."

Wow! That same evening he wrote the music! All in a day's work for Charles Austin Miles. Here we are, more than nine decades later, reaping the benefits! What is your heart's response to this story?

____

____

____

____

____

Now, go back and look at the lyrics (sing it again if you wish) with Mary Magdalene and Jesus in mind. Does this change your perspective?

____

____

____

____

____

This song often triggers a memory. (Perhaps it was played at a loved one's funeral. Maybe it reminds you of the rose petals pressed into your Aunt Ruth's Bible.) If this song triggers a memory for you share it here. (If you WANT to!)

____

____

____

____

____

____

____

____

____

____

Read John 20:1-18.

Slide your feet into Mary's sandals. Slip on her tunic and grab a hankie! Jot down notes as you go. For an added adrenaline rush, do this! Mark everything she did (verbs such as: saw, ran, cried, turned, wept, bent, looked, etc.) with a highlighter or better still, mark them in Lady BUG red! (If you don't enjoy marking in your Bible, you can make a list of those words below.) Do your best to see what Mary saw and feel what Mary felt. The more you put into this lesson, the more you'll get out of it. (Kinda like life, eh?!)

If you still have time and energy left, venture down a Lady BUG trail of your choice! Take a gander at the goodies past the Garden Gate! Perhaps today is the day to stop and smell the roses. (Hint: there is only one scripture in the NIV Bible that mentions a "rose." Scratch and sniff the scriptures 'til you find it. Where is it? What does the verse mean?) Did any other scriptures come to your mind while you were singing the song? Dig in the Word to find them! While you were reading John 20, did a question about Peter or John nudge its way into your noggin? Maybe the Spirit is moving you to respond in a different way altogether. Listen to that wee voice and **Write ON**...

Day 2: In the Garden

Snack to nibble on: John 19:41-42 At the place where Jesus was crucified, there was a garden, and in the garden a new tomb....they laid Jesus there.

Let's begin where Charles Austin Miles did. IN THE GARDEN.

What garden? There are several gardens mentioned in the Bible.
We know the **Garden of Eden** was planted by God (Genesis 2:8). God put Adam and Eve in this garden to work it and take care of it (Genesis 2:15) but then banished them from the garden (Genesis 3:23-24) after they sinned.

The **Garden of Gethsemane** (Matthew 26:36 and Mark 14:32) was a favorite meeting place for Jesus and His disciples. (John 18:1-2) Jesus was also betrayed and arrested in this garden.

Then, there's the **garden near Golgotha.** This is the garden we're interested in today! This is the garden we are singing about. This is the garden in which Jesus rose from the dead! Let's do a little digging in the Word and find out all we can about this special garden.

Read John 19:38-42.

Write verses 41-42 in the margin. Circle or highlight anything you find significant.

Golgotha (an Aramaic word) was the place where Jesus was crucified. It means The Place of the Skull. (See Matthew 27:33)

The garden was "nearby." (John 19:42) According to John 19:38, who asked Pilate for the body of Jesus? ________________________________

Why did Joseph keep his discipleship a secret?

____

In order to find out more about Joseph of Arimathea, let's look at the other gospel accounts.

Read Matthew 27:57-61. According to verse 57, Joseph was:

- ❑ a rich man
- ❑ a poor man

Zero in on verse 60. The new tomb was **his own** that he, himself, had cut out of the rock! Who rolled the big stone in front of the entrance to the tomb? In your opinion, why is this significant?

____

____

Who watched him do this? ________________________________
(Hang on to that thought. This will be important later!)

Now, let's read Mark's account and gather some more tidbits. **Read Mark 15:42-47.**

What was Joseph a member of? (v. 43) ________________________
(Note: the Council is also called the Sanhedrin)

What was Joseph waiting for? ______________________________

How did Joseph ask for Jesus' body?___________________________

Now, read Luke 23:50-56. What two adjectives does Luke use to describe Joseph in verse 50?

__________ and _______________.

In your own words, describe the importance of verse 51. Please use the margin and be specific!

Notice verse 53 tells us specifically about the tomb "one in which no one had yet been laid." Pay particular attention to verse 55. What did the group of women (which we know included Mary Magdalene) see?

____

____

Now, let's venture back to **John 19** and see what else we can learn. According to verse 39, who accompanied Joseph?

____

Let's find out who Nicodemus was and why he was helping Joseph bury Jesus! **Read John 3:1-21.**

Choose two. Nicodemus was:

- ❑ a Pharisee
- ❑ a Saducee
- ❑ a member of the Jewish Ruling Council
- ❑ a member of the Glee Club

What did Nicodemus know about Jesus? (v. 2)

____

When did Nicodemus come to question Jesus? (v. 2) Why do you think he chose to come then?

____

Pay close attention to John 3:14-15. Summarize what Jesus told Nicodemus.

____

____

____

I love knowing that Nicodemus' ears were the first to hear one of the most famous verses in the Bible. **John 3:16!** Perhaps you know this verse by heart! If so, quote it now. If not, read it from the text aloud. Drink in the fact that Jesus was speaking to Nicodemus in real time and to <u>us</u> now!

Write John 3:16 in the margin.

Read John 7:50-51. What does this passage show about the character of Nicodemus?

____

____

Based on everything you read about Nicodemus, why do you think he accompanied Joseph in preparing Jesus' body for burial?

____

____

Henry H. Halley had this to say about Nicodemus in *Halley's Bible Handbook*, "His coming out of the shadows in the hour of Jesus' humiliation, when even the Twelve had fled for cover, risking his own life on that final day, is one of the noblest incidents of Scripture!" [2]

Let's head back to the garden in **John 19**. Notice in verse 39 Nicodemus brought a mixture of myrrh and aloes, about seventy-five pounds! This was a HUGE amount usually only used in royal burials! [3] Joseph and Nicodemus worked together wrapping Jesus' body in strips of linen. Stop for a moment and picture the scene. On the day Jesus was born His mother, Mary, wrapped Him in "cloths." Now, 33 years later, His body was being wrapped in "cloths" again. How does this imagery speak to your heart?

____

____

It is intriguing to me that these two men had both been followers of Jesus "in secret" before His death. After His death, they both came out boldly to honor Jesus with tender loving care. Let's apply this to our lives today. What is the difference between honoring God "in secret" and honoring God "in public"? How do we practice both? Make suggestions in the margin.

We learned from Matthew and Mark's gospels that Joseph rolled a big stone in front of the entrance to the tomb. Remember who was watching?

____

Read Matthew 27:62-66. Why did the chief priests and the Pharisees want the tomb to be made secure?

____

____

According to verse 66, what two things did they do to ensure the tomb would be secure?

____

Read Luke 23:55-56. What did the women do after they left the tomb? What did they do on the Sabbath and why?

____

____

Read Mark 16:1. What did Mary Magdalene and the other women buy and what did they plan to do with their purchase?

____

____

Read Matthew 28:2-4. Who rolled back the stone? ____________________

Describe his appearance.

Describe the reaction of the guards.

Let's close our time together today reflecting upon the events that have taken place in the garden so far. Review your notes. Pray for God to give you an AHA moment! Did you learn something today that you didn't know before? Include ONE THING you Better Understand about God!

Day 3: Freshly-Dipped

Begin your study today pondering this thought-provoking poem by June Masters Bacher.

God handed me a morning
All freshly-dipped in dew
I said, "How shall I use it?"
He said, "It's up to you!"

Here's a fun fact! Did you know that ladybugs LOVE to drink the morning dew daily? Just a few drops will keep them hydrated for hours. Here's another fun fact! Roses are a ladybug's favorite flower!

Remember the first line of our Garden song?

I come to the garden alone,
while the _________ is still on the _______________.

Hmmm...how can we apply this to our daily routine?

____

____

____

____

____

____

____

According to the *Holman Bible Dictionary*, dew is "moisture that forms into drops of water on the earth during a cool night." [4] Dew is used in the Bible to symbolize many different things.

Read Genesis 27:27-28. (You'll have to use a few context clues to find out who Isaac is talking to.) How is **dew** used in this context?

____

____

____

Read Deuteronomy 32:1-4. Join Moses as he sings his song to the Israelites. What does **dew** symbolize in verse 2?

Read Judges 6:36-40. (You will remember this passage from our earlier study.) What does Gideon use to ask for divine revelation? How does God respond?

Read Psalm 133. Allow David to sing this pleasant song in your ear. Especially tune your ears when he sings verse 3. What does the **dew** represent in this context?

Read Proverbs 19:12. How is the king's favor described? Taking into account what we've already studied about God's "favor" what does this verse mean to you?

Have you ever tasted the soft drink Mountain Dew®? If so, do you like it? Why or why not? (If you've never tasted it run out and buy a can and take a sip. I'll wait right here! ☺)

Lady BUG trails

Through the years Mountain Dew® has had many ad slogans but my all-time favorite was their very first one! This ad campaign was launched in the mid-sixties (shortly after I was born, which was not long ago!). See if you like this slogan as much as I do.

"Ya-hoo, Mountain Dew. It'll tickle your innards!"

Considering everything we've learned about dew in the Word of God, I think this oldie but goodie slogan can certainly apply to our Christian lives! What do you think? No Rules...Just Write!

Read John 4:7-14. Summarize this in your own words.

Write the words of Christ from John 7:37-38. What does this mean to you?

If you want to, try this experiment. One day this week, get up very early in the morning, while it is still dark, and take a few sips of that DEW on the roses! What a refreshing way to start the day! Record the blessings you receive as a result.

Just DEW it! ☺

Lady BUG trails

Day 4: Morning Glory!

Snack to nibble on: John 20:1 Early on the first day of the week, while it was still dark, Mary Magdalene went to the tomb.

Remember on Day 1 of this chapter when we slid our feet into Mary's sandals and visited the tomb with her, complete with tunic and hankie? Today we're going back to John 20 so grab your magnifying glass to examine a few more details. Read John 20:1-2. What time of day did Mary Magdalene go to the tomb? ______________________

I love the phrase "while it was still dark." It reminds me of the "wife of noble character" in Proverbs 31 (see verse 15). Who else do we know and love who enjoyed getting up at this time of day? (Mark 1:35)______________

Chronologically, Mary Magdalene first appears in Scripture in the gospel of Luke during Jesus' second tour of Galilee. Magdalene is not Mary's "last name"; it simply tells us she was from Magdala in Galilee.[5].

Read Luke 8:1-3. From what had Mary been cured? ______________

How many demons had "come out" of her? ______________
We know from Mark 16:9 that Jesus Himself had exorcised those 7 demons! Imagine for a moment what life must have been like BC (before Christ!) for Mary. She must have felt tremendous gratitude toward Him. What a drastic change He had made in her life! Look closely at Luke 8:3. How did Mary Magdalene support Jesus and His disciples?______________

What do you think this means?

____

Matthew and Mark also tell us that Mary followed Jesus and "cared for His needs." (Mt. 27:55 and Mk. 15:41) In the margin, list some specific ways Mary may have cared for His needs.

Unfortunately, Mary Magdalene is not mentioned again by name in Scripture until the day we see her at Golgotha, watching her "miracle worker" being nailed to the cross. Likely, she was one of the women mentioned in Luke 23:27. What were the women doing?______________

What does this tell you about the relationship Jesus had with women?

____

According to John 20:2, Mary ran to Peter and John. What did she tell them?

____

____

Read John 20:3-10. Describe in your own words what happened. Who arrived at the tomb first? Who went in first? What did they see?

____

____

____

According to verse 10, where did Peter and John go?

____

Now, read John 20:11-17.

What was Mary doing while standing outside the tomb? ______________

Describe the scene in verse 12. Where were the angels sitting?

____

____

What did Mary think had happened to Jesus?

____

____

Consider this. Why did Mary jump to the conclusion that someone must have taken His body? Why did she not assume that He had risen from the dead? Record your thoughts in the margin.

Use your magnifying glass to take a closer look at verse 15. What does Jesus call her?

____

What two questions does He ask her?

1.

2.

Lady BUG trails

Lady BUG trails

Fill in the blanks from the latter half of verse 15. "Thinking he was the ______________________________..."

Yikes! Egad! And, Shazam! Why on earth do you think Mary would mistake the risen Savior as nothing more than a gardener?

____

____

Verse 16 is my favorite verse in the whole chapter. Let's write it in Big Bold letters.

Jesus said to her, "____________."

Notice that right after Jesus called her by name she did two things. List these in the margin.

She turned toward Him. This makes me think she must have been turned "away" from Him when she thought He was the gardener. What are your thoughts?

____

____

She cried out, "Rabboni!" How is this word translated in English?

____

We have one Teacher and that is Christ! (See Matthew 23:10.)

What an enormous lesson this is for us! Sometimes in our own lives we get confused and disoriented. We have a hard time seeing Christ in the chaos. Could it be that we have "turned away" from Him and that's why we don't notice that He's right there with us? IN US? Record your first thoughts in the margin. No Rules...Just Write!

Ladies, hear my whole heart on this deal. **God knows us by name**! All we have to do is listen for His voice - the voice of Truth - and run, run, run as fast as we can from all the other voices!

Read John 10:1-18. Pay close attention to verses 3-5. (How does the Good Shepherd call His own sheep?) Summarize these verses in your own words. Apply it to your own life.

Let's look at John 20:17 in the Amplified Bible.

> *Jesus said to her, "Do not cling to Me [do not hold Me], for I have not yet ascended to the Father. But go to My brethren and tell them, I am ascending to My Father and your Father, and to My God and your God."* ***John 20:17 (AMP)***

What do you think Jesus meant when He told Mary not to "cling" to Him?

This is just my opinion but I think perhaps Jesus was saying to Mary, "Don't cling to me as Jesus of the past...instead, proclaim the news about me as Jesus of the present and the future! I have risen! Go spread the news!"

I love the latter half of verse 17. Jesus makes sure Mary knows that God is **HER Father**, too! He makes sure Mary knows that God is **HER God**, too! How is this truth relevant to us today?

According to John 20:18, Mary went to the disciples and told them the great news. What did she tell them?

I have SEEN the Lord! What a declaration! Mary Magdalene has been called "the apostle to the apostles" because she had the unique honor of being the first one to SEE Jesus after He rose from the grave and had the privilege of telling the other apostles. Let's close our time together asking God to open the eyes of our hearts so that we, too, might SEE Him and proclaim the good news to others!

[1] Elvis Presley: Original Versions of Songs He Sang
[2] Halley, p. 693
[3] The NIV Study Bible, p. 1635
[4] Butler, p. 420
[5] The NIV Study Bible, p. 1553

Chapter 12:

Day 1: And He Walks With Me

Snack to nibble on: 2 Corinthians 6:16 (NIV) God said, "I will live with them and walk among them, and I will be their God, and they will be my people."

Let's begin by singing the chorus of "I Come to the Garden Alone." Sing it slowly and let the Spirit fill you!

And He walks with me, and He talks with me,
And He tells me I am His own;
And the joy we share as we tarry there,
None other has ever known.

Honestly, I have started and stopped...started and stopped...started and stopped this lesson at least six times! "I Come to the Garden Alone" has been ringing in my ears. The song is so appealing and yet, I want to know how to apply these beautiful words!

And He walks with me!

The very idea is fascinating on so many levels! What does this phrase mean to you? Jot your first response in the margin.

The idea of God walking with me is so intimate! Today, we're going to dig in the Word and see if we can unearth some treasures about this wonderful subject! First, let's look at what the Bible has to say about God "walking." Throughout the Bible we find figures of speech that attribute human characteristics to God, called anthropomorphisms. [1] Just for fun, read the following scriptures and circle God's "body parts."

Psalm 89:13	right hand	arm	neck	elbow
Psalm 33:6	nose	shoulder	feet	mouth
Psalm 34:15-16	eyes	chin	ears	face

Does God literally have arms, hands, eyes, ears, a mouth, and a face? Why do you think the psalmist describes God using this terminology?

____

Read Genesis 3:1-19. Verse 8 piques my curiosity! I wonder. What sound did God make as He "walked" in the garden? Did He choose the cool of the day because it was most comfortable to Him? If He walked in the garden back then, does He still "walk" in the garden today? Is this verse figurative or literal? Take a little time to ruminate and speculate! Write your questions or comments about this verse.

____

____

____

____

It seems silly to me that Adam and Eve would "hide" from God among the trees of the garden. Didn't they know Hide and Seek was (and still is) a futile game to play with God? In the margin, list some ways we attempt to "hide" from God today.

Take a moment to consider how very different history would have been if Adam and Eve had chosen to walk WITH God rather than run FROM God! Let's not make the same mistake today!

The Old Testament mentions a couple of men who chose to walk with God. We can read about their lives and discover the enormous benefits they received!

Read Genesis 5:21-27. Who was the father of Methuselah? How old was he when he became a father to Methuselah?

____

What did Enoch do after he became a father?

_ _ _ _ _ _   _ _ _ _   _ _ _ 300 years.

How long did Enoch live on the earth? ____________________

Write Genesis 5:24.

____

____

This passage is so rich in imagery! **Enoch walked with God!** This is the first time in Scripture the phrase "walked with God" is used. Let's examine this passage in the Amplified Bible.

> *And Enoch walked [in habitual fellowship] with God; and he was not, for God took him [home with Him]. Genesis 5:24 (AMP)*

He walked in habitual fellowship. Habitual means "done constantly or repeatedly." The word fellowship means "companionship; sharing similar interests or experiences." [2] We could say that Enoch made a HABIT of sharing companionship with God. Enoch constantly shared experiences with God. God's interests became Enoch's interests! The Hebrew word for "walked" in this context is *halak*. This word literally means "to walk, go, travel; to move to and fro, wander." By extension *halak* means "to walk as a lifestyle, a pattern of conduct." [3]

With these definitions in mind, how do you think Enoch "walked with God" and how can we do the same today? Ponder on paper in the margin!

Read Hebrews 11:1-5 in the NIV Bible.

According to verse 1, what is the definition of faith?

____

____

____

What did Enoch **NOT** experience? ________________________

Why was Enoch "commended" by God? (v. 5) __________________

Examine verse 6 carefully. What must we have in order to please God?

____

What 2 things must we **believe**?

that He ____________.

that He __________ those who earnestly __________ Him!

WOW! Believing God exists is one thing. Believing God rewards us when we earnestly seek Him is quite another! How does this truth speak to your heart?

____

____

Read 2 Corinthians 6:14-18. According to verse 16, what are believers?

____

We are the temple of the living God! When we choose to become Christians we are choosing to become a temple! God lives with us and walks among us! He is our God and we are His people! This is New Testament truth! Enoch paved the way by example. He habitually walked in fellowship with God for 300 years! He pleased God with his faith. Genesis 5:24 tells us that he "was no more, because God took him away." What does this phrase mean to you?

____

____

Enoch was certainly rewarded for his faith! Only one other man in Scripture (Elijah) had the privilege of being taken away to be with God without experiencing death. (See 2 Kings 2:11. This would make a great Lady BUG trail when you have time!)

Now, let's take a look at another man in Scripture that "walked with God." **Read Genesis 6:1-22.** Describe how God was feeling and why? (vv. 5-6)

____

____

In verses 8-9 we get to peer into a window of Noah's soul. Fill in the blanks.

Noah found __________in the eyes of the Lord...he was a

righteous man, ______________among the people of his time,

and he ___________ _________ ________!

Investigate the society in which Noah lived. Man's wickedness was great (v. 5) and the earth was corrupt and full of violence (v. 11). Even so, Noah remained blameless. Verse 22 says that Noah "did everything just as God commanded him." So, now we can add obedience to his list of attributes! How did Noah do it? In your opinion, what was Noah's secret recipe for righteousness? Create Noah's Secret Recipe in the margin.

Lady BUG trails

What does Hebrews 11:7 say about Noah? Chew on the little nuggets of truth you find. This verse is packed with them! Record what you want to remember.

___

___

It all boils down to one word: **CHOICE**. Noah <u>chose</u> to walk with God. He chose to build the ark in "holy fear" even though he had never seen rain before. Walking in "habitual fellowship" with God is a choice just like everything else! I believe the greatest gift God has ever given to us is our ability to choose! Adam and Eve were given choices and they blew it! Enoch and Noah chose to walk with God. Rack your brain about this. God is always willing to walk with us! It's our choice whether or not we are willing to walk with Him! Your thoughts?

___

___

___

The following verse is sooooooooooo important. Not only do we walk with Him but we also walk ***like*** Him! **Write 1 John 2:6.**

___

___

___

Let's close our day together with a time of reflection and prayer. Look back over your notes. In your own life, are you walking in habitual fellowship with God? If so, take this time to praise God for the intimacy you share. If not...perhaps this would be a great time to lace up your shoes and head to the garden alone for a nice, long walk!

Day 2: And He Talks With Me

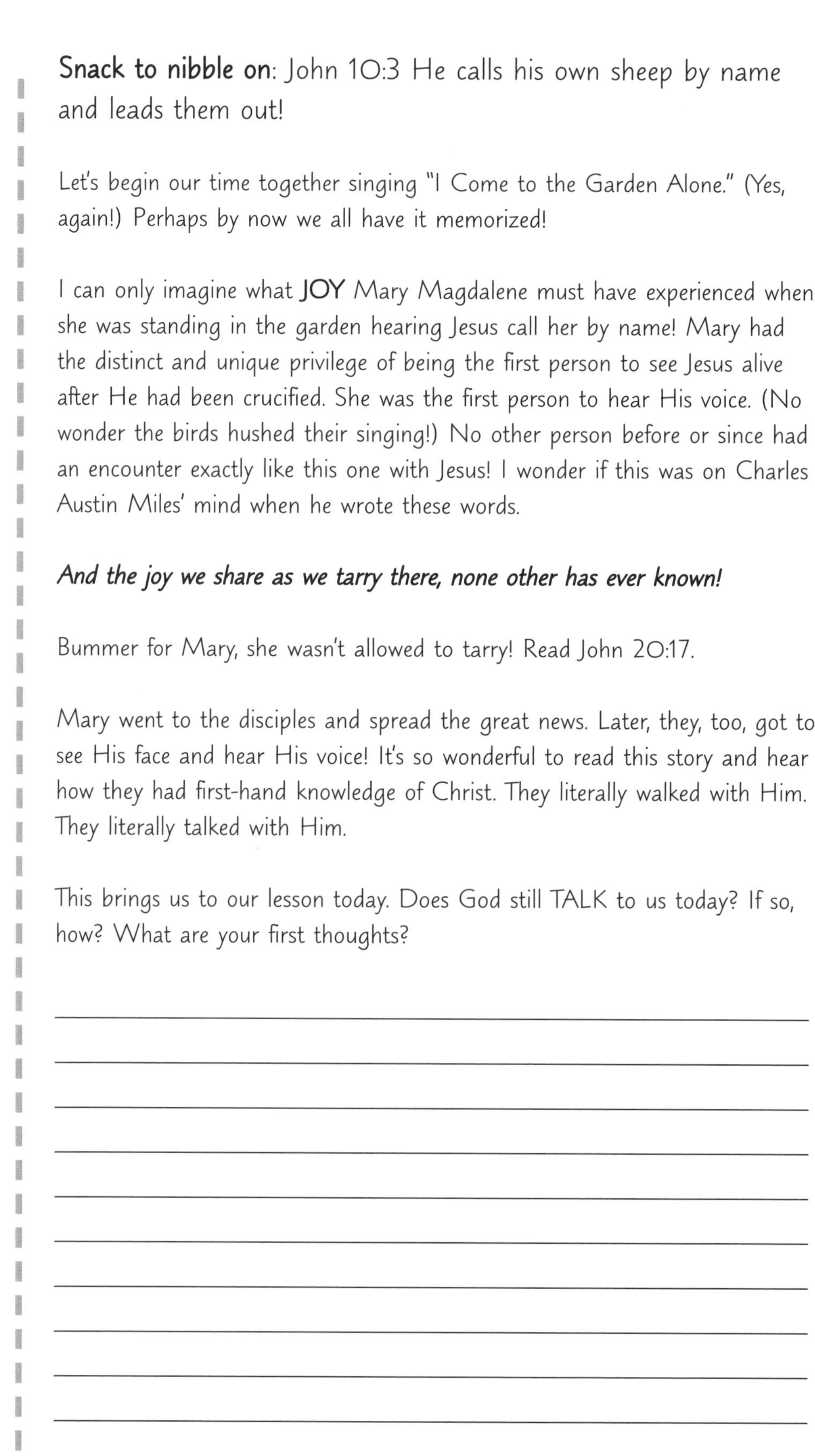

Snack to nibble on: John 10:3 He calls his own sheep by name and leads them out!

Let's begin our time together singing "I Come to the Garden Alone." (Yes, again!) Perhaps by now we all have it memorized!

I can only imagine what **JOY** Mary Magdalene must have experienced when she was standing in the garden hearing Jesus call her by name! Mary had the distinct and unique privilege of being the first person to see Jesus alive after He had been crucified. She was the first person to hear His voice. (No wonder the birds hushed their singing!) No other person before or since had an encounter exactly like this one with Jesus! I wonder if this was on Charles Austin Miles' mind when he wrote these words.

And the joy we share as we tarry there, none other has ever known!

Bummer for Mary, she wasn't allowed to tarry! Read John 20:17.

Mary went to the disciples and spread the great news. Later, they, too, got to see His face and hear His voice! It's so wonderful to read this story and hear how they had first-hand knowledge of Christ. They literally walked with Him. They literally talked with Him.

This brings us to our lesson today. Does God still TALK to us today? If so, how? What are your first thoughts?

In the Old Testament, God spoke with His people in many different ways.

Read Exodus 33:11-17. How did God speak to Moses?

What is your favorite part of this passage and why?

Oh...to have God say **"I am pleased with you and I know you by name!"** I get chills just thinking about it! What is your heart's response?

Read Psalm 16:7-11. Pay very close attention to verse 7. What happens to David at night?

How can we apply this to our daily lives?

Read Psalm 34:17-18. Write this passage in your own words and internalize the truth you find!

Lady BUG trails

Read Psalm 119:9-16. What do you want to remember about this passage?

Read Proverbs 2:6-8. Where do wisdom, knowledge, and understanding come from?

Take out your magnifying glass and read 1 John 3:24. How do we know that He lives in us?

Read Revelation 3:19-21. Write this passage in your own words.

How do we hear His voice today?

Read John 10:1-18. We have discussed this before but it is sooooooooo important I believe it bears repeating!!! How do the sheep know their shepherd?

What are some ways in our daily life that we can listen for His voice? What do we do when we hear our name being called?

What does verse 16 mean to you?

Read Psalm 29. Describe the voice of the Lord, according to David.

Read 1 Kings 19:9-18. Describe the voice of the Lord, according to Elijah.

Let's close our time together today by asking God to speak to us from His holy Word! **Read 1 Corinthians 2:1-16.** Let each truth sink in. Pour out your heart in prayer asking God to reveal His truth by His Spirit. Record what He teaches you. Praise Him for this wonderful form of communication!

Call to me and I will answer you!
I'll tell you marvelous and wondrous things that you could never figure out on your own. Jeremiah 33:3 (MSG)

Lady BUG trails

Day 3: Living the Lyrics: Ten Thousand Angels

Read Matthew 26:53. Skim the verses in context. Summarize in your own words what Jesus is saying.

____

____

Our song of the day is a bittersweet tale! We know the tale well! (Fortunately for us, we also know the rest of the story!) Even so, as you sing, visualize the scene. Stand at the cross. Sing from your heart.

Ten Thousand Angels

(Words and Music by Ray Overholt, 1959)

They bound the hands of Jesus in the garden where He prayed
They led Him thru the streets in shame
They spat upon the Savior so pure and free from sin
They said, "Crucify Him; He's to blame."

Upon His precious head they placed a crown of thorns
They laughed and said, "Behold the King!"
They struck Him and they cursed Him and mocked His holy name
All alone He suffered everything.

When they nailed Him to the cross, His mother stood nearby
He said, "Woman, behold thy son!"
He cried, "I thirst for water," but they gave Him none to drink
Then the sinful work of man was done.

To the howling mob He yielded, He did not for mercy cry
The cross of shame He took alone
And when He cried, "It's finished," He gave Himself to die
Salvation's wondrous plan was done.

He could have called ten thousand angels
To destroy the world and set Him free
He could have called ten thousand angels
But He died alone, for you and me!

It was Sunday morning; early service. She was sitting on her Daddy's lap. STILL (which is highly unusual) and PENSIVE. Lost in deep thought, she was staring into space, boring a hole into the pew in front of us. From the corner of my eye I could see that she had stopped singing. The rest of the congregation continued singing the last verse and then the refrain. She sat perfectly still...frozen in time.

As I closed the songbook I glanced over at her once more. By now, enormous "Alligator" tears had welled up in her almond-shaped eyes. I reached over and rubbed the palm of her hand, wondering what could possibly be rocking her seven-year-old world to such a degree. As she turned her face toward me, the tears began to trickle down her cheeks. She leaned over and whispered in my ear, *"Mommy, that's the saddest song I've ever heard! It makes me feel...so...sad inside!"*

At first I was puzzled; complete with furrowed brows. Then, from out of nowhere, clarity rang like a bell. **I understood!** She'd been listening to the lyrics! She had allowed the truth of the song to "rock her world" and her tears were quite a testimony to me! You see, we were about to take communion so the song leader had selected hymn #349 ("Ten Thousand Angels") to "prepare our minds." Her mind had been "prepared" all right! By this time she was hanging on to me with all her might. In an effort to console her I said, "Yes, Sweetie, that song is sad. Jesus did die alone for you and me. But, the greatest part of all is that he rose again!"

She considered this for a moment (having heard it many times before) and seemed to be processing what this ***really*** meant. She wiped a tear from her cheek and said, "I know. But, where is He NOW?" I pulled her into my lap and began stroking her hair. Thoughts of what I was "supposed" to say swirled around in my head. "Jesus is up in heaven sitting at the right hand of God," I managed to say softly.

"When is He coming back to get us?" she asked without skipping a beat. "I don't know, Sweetheart. Nobody knows." I answered. She held on to my neck for a few seconds with one hand and wiped the rest of her tears with the other. Then, she whispered some precious words that I'll not soon forget! **"Mommy, I sure hope He comes back soon, 'cause I can't WAIT to go to heaven with Him!"**

Lady BUG trails

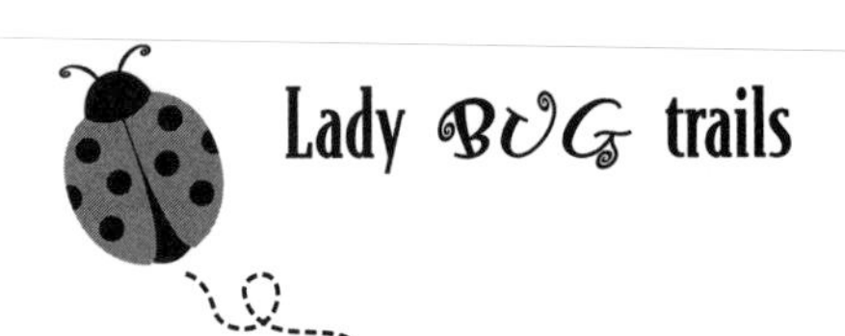

Does this touch your heart as it did mine? Do you have a similar story to share?

____

____

____

____

____

____

Children make the best teachers! I am reminded of what Jesus said in Matthew 18. Read verses 1-4.

What did the disciples ask Jesus? (v.1)

____

____

Jesus, in His infinite wisdom, did not answer with mere words. He chose to answer with an object lesson! Our creative Christ used a living, breathing "prop" that they could all relate to. Who did He call to participate in this lesson?

____

Place a bookmark in Matthew and let's compare Mark's account of this same event. Read Mark 9:33-36.

What question did Jesus ask His disciples? Why did they keep quiet?

____

____

____

____

I believe this piece of information is vital! They were not simply asking Jesus a philosophical question about greatness, they were ARGUING about who was the greatest! Silly men, did they really think they could keep their argument a secret? Thanks to Dr. Luke's account of this same story, we can be privy to one more crucial detail! Fill in the blanks from Luke 9:47 in the NIV Bible.

Jesus, __ __ __ __ __ __ __ __ their __ __ __ __ __ __ __ __, took a little __ __ __ __ __ and had him stand beside him. (Luke 9:47 NIV)

I'm not sure why this verse pole-vaulted itself right off the page and into my heart, but it most certainly did. Now, the verse is running laps around the track in my mind! Jesus knew their thoughts! In 1 Chronicles 28:9 David reminds his son Solomon that the LORD searches every heart and understands every motive behind the thoughts! Woo Woo! Perhaps the scenario in Capernaum had more to do with the disciples' motives than anything else. What is your opinion?

____

____

____

Mark 9:36 says Jesus took the child in His arms! (That's one more reason to become like a child! Safe in the arms of Jesus – that's where I want to be!) Why do you suppose He did this?

____

____

____

Rewind to Matthew 18. Write verse 3 from the NIV Bible here.

____

____

____

____

____

I highly recommend making a Lady BUG Fast Food card out of this verse! The first five words comfort me to my core! He told them the truth. (He tells us the truth, too. EVERY TIME!) Truth for the disciples involved changing and becoming! Listen to the Words of Christ from The Amplified Bible. Believe that He is speaking them directly to YOU today!

> "Truly I say to you, unless you repent [change, turn about] and become like little children [trusting, lowly, loving, forgiving], you can never enter the kingdom of heaven [at all]. Whoever will humble himself therefore and become like this little child [trusting, lowly, loving, forgiving] is greatest in the kingdom of heaven. And whoever receives and accepts and welcomes one little child like this for My sake and in My name receives and accepts and welcomes Me."
> (Matthew 18:3-5 AMP)

Lady BUG trails

Summarize that passage in your own words and personalize it to fit your unique situation.

I want to change and become like my precious little girl. I want to humble myself enough to have tears of compassion running down my face when singing or reading about the suffering of Christ! I want to be MOVED inside and out, just as Jesus was on so many occasions! (While taking a Lady BUG trail this week, make a rest stop at Compassion Cul-De-Sac! See how many New Testament scriptures you can find that contain the phrase "He had compassion on them!")

Spend your Quiet Time today doing just that - being QUIET. Light a candle. Put on some classical music. Quietly and compassionately contemplate Christ's gift. Read the story of Christ's crucifixion in the gospels. You can choose your favorite account or read them all! But, before you read these events, remember the words of Jesus. Change! Become like a little child. Humble yourself enough to be MOVED.

Matthew 27:33-56

Mark 15:22-41

Luke 23:33-49

John 19:17-37

He could have called ten thousand angels ...but He chose to die for YOU! Use this page during your Quiet Time in any way your heart and soul desires to reflect on what you read about the crucifixion.

Day 4: Living the Lyrics: He LIVES!

Lady BUG trails

We have studied about the events that took place in the garden near Golgotha. We have gotten to know Joseph of Arimathea and Nicodemus. We went to the garden with Mary Magdalene while the dew was still on the roses and witnessed our risen Savior call her by name!!! We have analyzed what it means to walk with Him and talk with Him. So, this brings us to the question, "What now?"

What does all of this mean to us in our daily walk with God in the 21st Century? My friend and fellow philosopher Brian Shrock taught our Sunday school class recently. He stood before us, held his Bible in the air, looked out into our faces and said,

"So What?"

I have to admit, we were all a bit stunned. You could have heard a pin drop. Looking around the room, we each wondered who would be the first brave soul to answer THAT question. Eyebrows sent non-verbal messages, "Is he being serious? Should we laugh or be as somber as possible? Do we have a clue where he's going with this?" I've thought about it almost every day since then. If you'd been sitting in the classroom, how would you have answered?

____

____

____

____

____

____

Honestly, that question has changed the way I study the Bible. Brian recommended that we apply the "So What?" test to every passage of scripture we read. "So what does this mean to me? How does this apply to my life?" If the Bible does not directly affect the way we live our lives, it might as well just be another good ole history book! He encouraged us to assume that EVERY verse in the Word of God contains something we've never seen before, no matter how many times we've read it! This simple statement has prompted me to ask God to open my eyes to something new every day!

Let's return to the chorus of "I Come to the Garden Alone." By now, I'm sure you know it by heart.

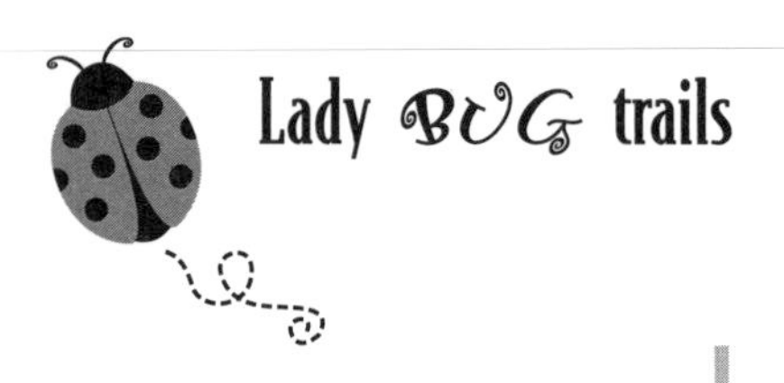

And He walks with me, and He talks with me
And He tells me I am His own;
And the joy we share as we tarry there,
None other has ever known!

Complete this truth from Isaiah 43:1 in the NIV Bible.

"Fear not, for I have ________________ you;

I have summoned you ______ ____________;

You are _______________!

Lady BUG Sisters, do you believe what you just wrote? Are you filled with JOY about that truth?

____

____

____

Read Galatians 3:13-14.

What did Christ redeem us from? Why did He redeem us?

____

____

____

____

____

According to verse 14, what do we receive by faith? What does this mean to you?

____

____

____

____

Before singing the song for today, read the phenomenal lyrics loud. Allow the truth in this story to fall on you like DEW. (It'll tickle your innards! ☺) Become 7 years old again. Permission is granted to DELIGHT YOURSELF IN THE LORD (Psalm 37:4) in whatever way you choose! After reading the lyrics go back and sing the song.

Lady BUG trails

He Lives

(Words and Music by A.H. Ackley, 1933)

I serve a risen Savior He's in the world today
I know that He is living, whatever men may say
I see His hand of mercy, I hear His voice of cheer
And just the time I need Him He's always near.

In all the world around me I see His loving care
And tho my heart grows weary I never will despair
I know that He is leading thru all the stormy blasts
The day of His appearing will come at last

Rejoice, rejoice, O Christian
Lift up your voice and sing
Eternal hallelujahs to Jesus Christ the King!
The hope of all who seek Him
The help of all who find
None other is so loving so good and kind.

He lives, He lives, Christ Jesus lives today!
He walks with me
And talks with me along life's narrow way!
He lives, He lives, salvation to impart!
You ask me how I know He lives?
He lives within my heart!

Now, here comes the question. Are you ready? So What? How does each and every line of this song affect your life? Does the truth in this song affect your choices? Does the fact that HE LIVES dramatically change the way you live?

____

____

____

____

Lady BUG Sisters, this song is what the Christian life is all about. It is steeped in truth from the Scriptures. Do you believe that Jesus Christ, the Son of God, died on the cross for **YOU**? Do you believe He rose again? Do you believe HE LIVES today? Have you made a personal decision to follow Him? Have you been baptized in His name? (See Acts 2:38 and Mark 16:16.) If so, when? What are the details of your conversion? If not, do you have a reason for waiting? Explore that honestly here.

Spend the remainder of your time today pouring out your heart in prayer to our Almighty God. Let your "little girl within" climb into your Father's lap and tell Him how much you appreciate the sacrifice He and His Son made for YOU! There's soooooooo much to say. Begin right away!

Write 1 John 4:16.

Amen and Amen!

[1] Morris
[2] Ibid
[3] Goodrick, p. 1394

Happy Trails to You!

Our main goal for this Bible Study was Better Understanding God. Do you feel that you understand Him better?

____

____

I'm a little sad today knowing this will be our last trail together (until we meet again!). But, my heart is filled with JOY knowing that our journey has just begun! It warms my heart to think about all you ladies out there. Let's call ourselves **Lady BUGs Living the Lyrics and Loving the Lord!** ☺ Please take these reminders with you as you continue to blaze the trail toward better understanding Him.

1. When God says Go, You Go Girl!
2. Know without a doubt who you are and WHOSE you are!
3. Take a deep Breath of God and say, "Ahhh!"
4. Always remember that Truth is Good Food! Take TIME to pig out on His smorgasbord daily!
5. Do Not Be Afraid! Choose to listen and believe the Voice of Truth!
6. Savor the Favor! His Amazing Grace is a marvelous flavor!
7. Ponder in your heart the Great Things He has done for you!
8. Choose Peace in the Chaos! Others will see the Light of the world inside of you!
9. Strain those "peas" out of your river and ask God to "double-dip" you in His chocolate fountain of JOY!
10. Thronging burdens pressing? Choose Peace Squared!
11. Go to the garden while the dew is still on the roses. (No more excuses... Just DEW it!) ☺
12. Walk and talk with the Gardener! Lean in. Hear Him whisper, "You are mine!" Spread the Good News to everyone you meet, "He Lives!"

Bibliography

Acronym Finder. (2005). Retrieved June, 2005, from http://acronyms.thefreedictionary.com/Being+Under+Satan's+Yoke

Bailey, A. E. (1950). *The Gospel in Hymns: Backgrounds and Interpretations.* New York: Charles Scribner's Sons.

Baker, W., & Carpenter, E. (Eds.). (2003). *The Complete Word Study Dictionary: Old Testament.* Chattanooga, Tennessee: AMG Publishers.

Barclay, W. (1953). *The Gospel of Luke.* Philadelphia: The Westminster Press.

Butler, T. C., Brand, C., Draper, C., England, A., Bond, S., & Clendenen, E. R. (Eds.). (2003). *Holman Illustrated Bible Dictionary* (Rev. ed.). Nashville, Tennessee: Holman Bible Publishers.

Cardiopulmonary resuscitation. (2005). In *Encyclopaedia Britannica Online.* Retrieved June 8, 2005, from http://www.britannica.com/eb/article-9020301

Churchill, W. *Quotation Search - Quote Search - The Quotations Page:.* Retrieved September, 2006, from http://www.quotationspage.com/search.php3?Search=truth&startsearch=Search&Author=churchill&C=mgm&C=motivate&C=classic&C=coles&C=poorc&C=lindsly

Dockrey, K., Godwin, J., & Godwin, P. (Eds.). (2000). *The Student Bible Dictionary.* Uhrichsville, Ohio: Barbour.

Dykes, D. (2004, May 30). Thumbnails of Truth, #1046, *Part 19 in the "Aliens" series.* Tyler, Texas: Discover Life Ministries.

Eisenberg, A., Eisenberg Murkoff, H., & Hathaway, S. E. (1984). *What to Expect When You're Expecting.* New York: Workman Publishing Company.

Elvis Presley: Original Versions of Songs He Sang. (2006, August 22). Retrieved September, 2006, from http://users.pandora.be/davidneale/elvis/originals/list5.html

Favor. (n.d.). The American Heritage® Dictionary of the English Language, Fourth Edition. Retrieved June 28, 2005, from Dictionary.com website: http://dictionary.reference.com/search?q=favor&x=20&y=15

Gill, J. (1999). Commentary on 1 Peter 1:8. *The New John Gill Exposition of the Entire Bible.* Retrieved September, 2006, from http://www.searchgodsword.org/com/geb/view.cgi?book=1pe&chapter=001&verse=008

Gill, J. (1999). *Commentary on Ezekiel 16:4. The New John Gill Exposition of the Entire Bible.* Retrieved July, 2005, from http://www.studylight.org/com/geb/view.cgi?book=eze&chapter=016&verse=004

Gill, J. (1999). Commentary on Jeremiah 33:6. *The New John Gill Exposition.* Retrieved July, 2005, from http://www.searchgodsword.org/com/geb/view.cgi?book=jer&chapter=033&verse=006

Goodrick, E. W., & Kohlenberger Iii, J. R. (1999). *The Strongest NIV Exhaustive Concordance* (Rev. ed.). Grand Rapids, Michigan: Zondervan.

Hail Mary pass - Wikipedia, the free encyclopedia. (2006, August 8). Retrieved June, 2005, from http://en.wikipedia.org/wiki/Hail_Mary_pass

Halley, H. H. (2000). *Halley's Bible Handbook with the New International Version* (Rev. ed.). Grand Rapids, Michigan: Zondervan.

Hindson, E., & Dobson, E. (Eds.). (1999). "Yoked" With Jesus. *The Knowing Jesus Study Bible* (p. 1279). Grand Rapids, Michigan: Zondervan.

Japanese Culture and Daily Life. (2006, June 23). Retrieved May 4, 2005, from http://www.tjf.or.jp/eng/content/japaneseculture/02kutsu.htm Original Text: The Japan Forum Newsletter no8 "A day in The Life" June 1997.

John Newton - The Reformed Reader. (2006, September 4). Retrieved September 22, 2006, from http://www.reformedreader.org/rbb/newton/neindex.htm

The John Newton Project; Introduction. (2006, September). Retrieved September 22, 2006, from http://www.johnnewton.org/group/group.aspx?id=32663

Keller, P. (1970). Thou Anointest My Head With Oil. *A Shepherd Looks At Psalm 23* (pp. 111-124). Grand Rapids, Michigan: Zondervan.

Lucado, M. (1993). Forever Young. *He Still Moves Stones* (pp. 72-79). Dallas: Word Publishing.

Metcalf, L. T., & Simon, T. (2002). *Writing the Mind Alive, The Proprioceptive Method for Finding Your Authentic Voice.* New York: Ballantine.

Mikkelson, B. (2004, January 24). *Urban Legends Reference Pages: Religion (Amazing Grace).* Retrieved September, 2006, from http://www.snopes.com/religion/amazing.htm

Mondegreen. (2005). In *Wikipedia, the free encyclopedia:.* Retrieved July, 2005, from http://en.wikipedia.org/wiki/Mondegreen

Moore, D. T. (2001). Why Cant You Be Normal...Like Me? [CD]. Palm Desert, California: Moore On Life.

Morris, W. (Ed.). (1978). *The American Heritage Dictionary of the English Language, New College Edition* (Rev. ed.). Boston: Houghton Mifflin Company.

Newton, J. (1979). *Olney Hymns.* Olney, Buckinghamshire, England: Cowper and Newton Museum. Retrieved September, 2006, from http://www.ccel.org/ccel/newton/olneyhymns.txt reprinted 1984; public domain

The NIV Study Bible. (1985). Grand Rapids, Michigan: Zondervan Bible Publishers.

Peace, Perfect Peace. Retrieved July, 2005, from http://www.cyberhymnal.org/htm/p/e/peaceper.htm

Rogers, A. (2006, February 10). *Amazing Grace: The Story of John Newton.* Retrieved September 20, 2006, from http://www.texasfasola.org/biographies/johnnewton.html reprinted from the July-August 1996 issue of Away Here in Texas.

Seagraves, S. (2001, May 13). *Ladybug Lore.* Retrieved April, 2005, from http://www.geocities.com/sseagraves/ladybuglore.htm

Thayer And Smith. Greek Lexicon entry for Hagiazo. In *The New Testament Greek Lexicon.* Retrieved July, 2005, from http://www.searchgodsword.org/lex/grk/view.cgi?number=37

Vine, W. E., Unger, M. F., & White, Jr., W. (Eds.). (1996). *Vine's Complete Expository Dictionary of Old and New Testament Words.* Nashville: Thomas Nelson Publishers.

Virgin Mary grilled cheese sold for $28,000 - Peculiar Postings - MSNBC.com. (2004, November 23). Retrieved June, 2005, from http://www.msnbc.msn.com/id/6511148

Wheaties, The Breakfast of Champions. (2005,) Minneapolis, MN, General Mills Cereals, LLC, Retrieved June 2005, from Wheaties box.

Wilson, R. F. *Amazing Grace, the story of John Newton - Christian Articles Archive.* Retrieved September, 2006, from http://www.joyfulheart.com/misc/newton.htm

Zodhiates, S., Baker, W., & Hadjiantoniou, G. (Eds.). (1992). *The Complete Word Study Dictionary: New Testament* (Rev. ed.). Chattanooga, Tennessee: AMG International, Inc.

Lady BUG trails

Lady BUG trails

Lady BUG trails

Lady BUG trails

Lady BUG trails

Lady BUG trails

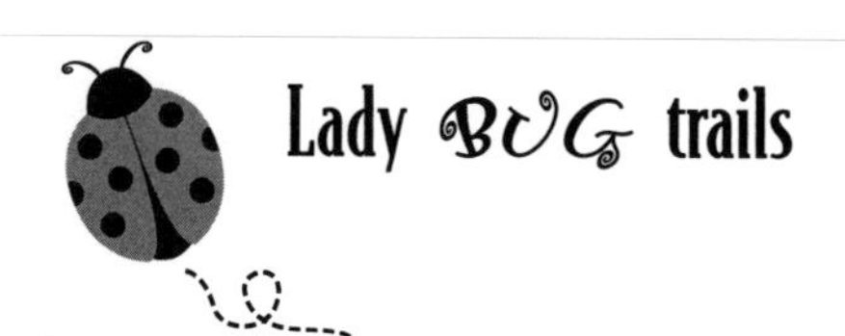
Lady BUG trails